Target
Get back on track

GRADE 5

Edexcel GCSE (9–1)
Spanish

Reading

Ana Kolkowska and Libby Mitchell

P Pearson

Published by Pearson Education Limited, 80 Strand, London, WC2R ORL

www.pearsonschoolsandfecolleges.co.uk

Copies of official specifications for all Pearson qualifications may be found on the website: qualifications.pearson.com

Text © Pearson Education Ltd 2018
Produced by Out of House Publishing
Typeset by Newgen KnowledgeWorks Pvt. Ltd., Chennai, India

The rights of Ana Kolkowska and Libby Mitchell to be identified as authors of this work have been asserted by them in accordance with the Copyright, Designs and Patents Act 1988.

First published 2018

21 20 19 18
10 9 8 7 6 5 4 3 2

British Library Cataloguing in Publication Data
A catalogue record for this book is available from the British Library.

ISBN 978 0435 18905 1

Printed in Slovakia by Neografia

Note from the publisher
Pearson has robust editorial processes, including answer and fact checks, to ensure the accuracy of the content in this publication, and every effort is made to ensure this publication is free of errors. We are, however, only human, and occasionally errors do occur. Pearson is not liable for any misunderstandings that arise as a result of errors in this publication, but it is our priority to ensure that the content is accurate. If you spot an error, please do contact us at resourcescorrections@pearson.com so we can make sure it is corrected.

This workbook has been developed using the Pearson Progression Map and Scale for Spanish.

To find out more about the Progression Scale for Spanish and to see how it relates to indicative GCSE 9–1 grades go to www.pearsonschools.co.uk/ProgressionServices

Helping you to formulate grade predictions, apply interventions and track progress.

Any reference to indicative grades in the Pearson Target Workbooks and Pearson Progression Services is not to be used as an accurate indicator of how a student will be awarded a grade for their GCSE exams.

You have told us that mapping the Steps from the Pearson Progression Maps to indicative grades will make it simpler for you to accumulate the evidence to formulate your own grade predictions, apply any interventions and track student progress. We're really excited about this work and its potential for helping teachers and students. It is, however, important to understand that this mapping is for guidance only to support teachers' own predictions of progress and is not an accurate predictor of grades.

Our Pearson Progression Scale is criterion referenced. If a student can perform a task or demonstrate a skill, we say they are working at a certain Step according to the criteria. Teachers can mark assessments and issue results with reference to these criteria which do not depend on the wider cohort in any given year. For GCSE exams however, all Awarding Organisations set the grade boundaries with reference to the strength of the cohort in any given year. For more information about how this works please visit: https://qualifications.pearson.com/en/support/support-topics/results-certification/understanding-marks-and-grades.html/Teacher

Contents

1 Recognising and understanding core vocabulary

This unit will help you learn how to recognise and understand the vocabulary that you need to answer the exam question. The skills that you will build are to:

- recognise common words
- show understanding of common words once you have recognised them
- take account of the context when showing understanding of common words.

In the exam, you will be asked to do reading tasks similar to the one below. This unit will prepare you to tackle these questions and choose or come up with the best answers.

1. For this exam task you first need to identify vocabulary for expressing opinions. Circle Ⓐ the eight words and phrases that introduce an opinion.

Don't answer this exam-style question yet. You will be asked to come back to it at the end of the unit.

Exam-style question

Holidays and travel

Read the opinions about types of holidays on a website forum.

Miguel:	Prefiero pasar las vacaciones en la costa, dado que me encanta ir de pesca y nadar en el mar. Si hace viento, también hago vela.
Susana:	Me gustan los hoteles lujosos con diversas tiendas y restaurantes con aire acondicionado. Prefiero no salir del hotel, si es posible.
Juan:	Me encanta ir al extranjero. Hago fotos y pruebo la cocina tradicional. Cuando hay alguna fiesta, me lo paso bomba.
Amelia:	Para mí es importante estar al aire libre, por eso siempre hago camping. También es divertido montar a caballo y hacer senderismo.

Who says what about their holiday preferences? Enter **Miguel**, **Susana**, **Juan** or **Amelia**.
You can use each person more than once.

Example: _Miguel_____ is sporty.

(a) .... likes discovering different cultures. (1)

(b) .... likes the beach. (1)

(c) .... enjoys partying. (1)

(d) .... thinks comfort is important. (1)

(e) .... likes the countryside. (1)

(f) .... doesn't like exploring. (1)

(6 marks)

To answer this question, it's important not just to recognise the words for places, but also to understand the words for activities to do with those places.

(2) Scan the text below. Underline Ⓐ the four places and circle Ⓐ the six activities mentioned in the text.

Do not answer this exam-style question yet. You will be asked to come back to it at the end of the unit.

Exam-style question

On holiday

Read Antonio's note below.

> Por la mañana
>
> Al castillo antes de comprar la entrada al estadio para ver el partido mañana. Luego comprar comida para la merienda en la playa.
>
> Por la tarde
>
> Tomar un refresco después de tomar el sol. Volver al albergue para ducharme. Comprar recuerdos para la familia.

Complete the gap in each sentence using a word from the box below. There are more words than gaps.

> museum   supermarket   ~~castle~~   sports centre   ice cream shop   guest house
>
> post office   stadium   bar   hostel   souvenir shop   tourist office

Example: Before buying his ticket, Antonio goes to the ___castle___ .

(a) To organise his trip to see the game, he needs to go to the .... (1)

(b) To prepare for the beach, he will need to go to the .... (1)

(c) After sunbathing, he will go to the .... (1)

(d) In the afternoon he will return to the .... (1)

(e) After showering, he will go to the .... (1)

(5 marks)

The three key questions in the **skills boosts** will help you improve how you answer these types of questions.

 1 How do I recognise common words?

 2 How do I show understanding of common words?

 3 How do I take account of the context of common words?

> **1** How do I recognise common words?

It's a good idea to learn words in blocks related to topic areas. It also helps to associate nouns with certain verbs. That way, when you read an exam text, you will be able to recognise and understand words in relation to each other.

Here are some typical exam-style statements. Before answering the questions on them, make sure you know your core vocabulary on the topic of holidays.

Lucía: Prefiero viajar en tren porque tengo miedo de volar. Además, me gusta ver el paisaje.

Julio: Quiero reservar una habitación con vistas al mar y media pensión.

Beatriz: Me alojo en un camping porque es más barato que un hotel.

Marcos: No me importa el frío. Me encanta la nieve y quiero aprender a esquiar.

---

1 Look at this list of holiday vocabulary. Match the Spanish to the English words. Write a letter next to each letter.

| A albergue juvenil | B avión | C visitar | D recuerdos | E viajar | F comprar |
| G castillo | H alojarse | I alquilar | J coche | K equipaje | L perder |

a rent _I_

b souvenirs ....

c car ....

d youth hostel ....

e lose ....

f buy ....

g stay ....

h plane ....

i travel ....

j castle ....

k visit ....

l luggage ....

2 Now look at these words from **1**. On paper, choose other words from the box above to create groups of related words. Use this technique to learn vocabulary in different topic groups.

Example: albergue juvenil _alojarse_

a avión

b visitar

c recuerdos

d alquilar

e equipaje

Remember that different words may be used to express the same thing. Think of **related vocabulary** to help you answer a question (*dinero: el precio, el coste, caro, barato, la tarjeta de crédito, el banco, costar*).

To help you learn vocabulary you can also try grouping words with the **same stem** (*el alojamiento – alojarse, la visita – visitar*), or with their **opposites** (*caro – barato, frío – calor*).

3 **a** Look again at the statements at the top of the page. Circle the key words in the Spanish texts which relate to each of the opinions in English in **b** below.

b Read the statements again. Who says what? Write the names in the gaps. You can use each person more than once.

Example: _Julio_ likes a nice view.

i .... wants to save money.

ii .... doesn't like planes.

iii .... would like a winter holiday.

iv .... prefers to eat dinner at the hotel.

How do I show understanding of common words?

Once you've recognised common vocabulary in an exam text, you need to make sure you choose the answers which show your understanding. Reading the texts and questions carefully and using your knowledge of common words will help you find the right answer.

① ⓐ Read the Spanish sentences and the English sentences in ⓑ. Notice that the key words in the English sentences are all places in a town. In the Spanish sentences, underline Ⓐ the key words related to the places mentioned in the English ones. Then annotate 🖉 them in English to show how they relate to a place.

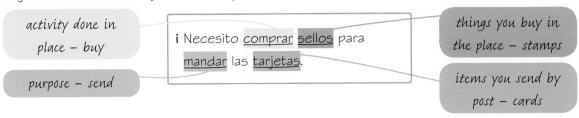

activity done in place – buy

i Necesito comprar sellos para mandar las tarjetas.

purpose – send

things you buy in the place – stamps

items you send by post – cards

ii Esta tarde vamos al partido y antes tengo que comprar las entradas.

iii Tengo que comprar crema solar para ir a la playa porque no quiero quemarme.

iv Primero pierdo el pasaporte y luego pierdo la cartera. ¡Qué desastre!

v Mi alojamiento tiene una piscina climatizada y dos restaurantes.

vi Necesito un plano del pueblo y un folleto sobre los lugares de interés.

ⓑ Now write 🖉 the letter of the correct Spanish sentence in ⓐ for each English statement.

Example: I want to go to the chemist. _iii_

A I'm going to the stadium later today. ....

B I need to find a post office. ....

C There is a tourist information office next door. ....

D Is there a police station nearby? ....

E I'm staying at a nice hotel. ....

Use the words that you are familiar with to help you understand the gist of the text and you'll find that unfamiliar words won't affect your answer. You may even be able to guess their meaning by placing them in context.

③ How do I take account of the context of common words?

When reading a Spanish text, use grammatical clues to help you understand a word in context and to answer a question.

> Always look carefully at prepositions as their use can alter the meaning of a sentence and they can mean different things in different contexts.
>
> | | | |
> |---|---|---|
> | *a* = to, at | *por* = through, for, to, by | *en* = in, on, at |
> | *de* = of, from, to | *para* = in order to, for | |

① Read the Spanish sentences and underline Ⓐ the correct translation of each preposition.

a El recepcionista habla de los clientes.　　The receptionist talks about / to the clients.

b El tren sale para Madrid.　　The train leaves from / for Madrid.

c Compro el recuerdo por mi abuela.　　I'm buying the souvenir on behalf of / for my grandmother.

d El museo abre desde las 9h.　　The museum is open from / at 9am.

e El bañador está en la maleta.　　The swimsuit is on / in the suitcase.

> Look carefully at tenses and verb endings, as well as prepositions, plus pronouns and adjective agreement, as these can also help you understand the context of words. (You'll get more practice on this in Unit 5.)

② Read these English and Spanish sentences and write ✏️ the letter for the Spanish sentence that best conveys the meaning of the English sentence in each case. Annotate ✏️ the sentences to help you work out the correct answer, as in the example.

Example: I go to the post office to post my cards. _B_

A | Voy a mandar las tarjetas por correo.

　immediate future　preposition 'by'　post

B | Voy a correos a mandar las tarjetas.

　present tense　preposition '(in order) to'

a I'm attending a sailing club for beginners. ....

A | Lo principal es empezar una clase de vela.

B | Asisto a una clase de vela para principiantes.

b I love Spanish cooking. ....

A | Me apasiona la cocina española.

B | Le entusiasma la cocina española.

c All the rooms have new hair dryers. ....

A | Hay un secador nuevo en mi habitación.

B | Las habitaciones tienen secadores nuevos.

Your turn!

Here is an exam-style question which requires you to put into practice the skills you have worked on, specifically showing understanding of common words once you have recognised them.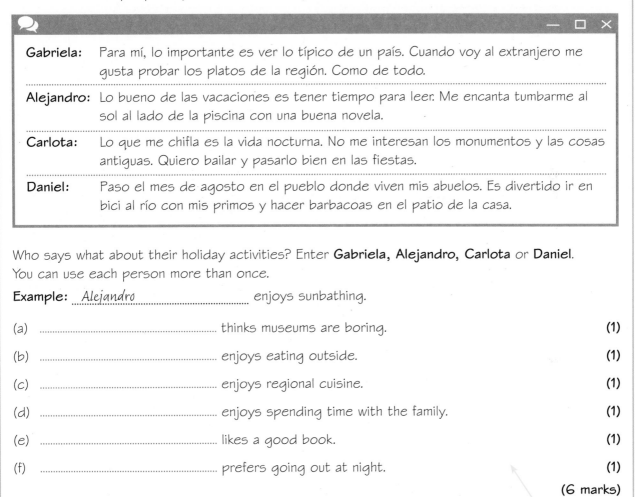

Exam-style question

Travel

Read what these people say about their holiday activities on a website forum.

Gabriela:	Para mí, lo importante es ver lo típico de un país. Cuando voy al extranjero me gusta probar los platos de la región. Como de todo.
Alejandro:	Lo bueno de las vacaciones es tener tiempo para leer. Me encanta tumbarme al sol al lado de la piscina con una buena novela.
Carlota:	Lo que me chifla es la vida nocturna. No me interesan los monumentos y las cosas antiguas. Quiero bailar y pasarlo bien en las fiestas.
Daniel:	Paso el mes de agosto en el pueblo donde viven mis abuelos. Es divertido ir en bici al río con mis primos y hacer barbacoas en el patio de la casa.

Who says what about their holiday activities? Enter **Gabriela, Alejandro, Carlota** or **Daniel**. You can use each person more than once.

Example: ...Alejandro... enjoys sunbathing.

(a) .... thinks museums are boring. (1)

(b) .... enjoys eating outside. (1)

(c) .... enjoys regional cuisine. (1)

(d) .... enjoys spending time with the family. (1)

(e) .... likes a good book. (1)

(f) .... prefers going out at night. (1)

(6 marks)

Rather than looking for direct translations of the questions in English, find vocabulary associated with the key words. In the example question, we can see that Alejandro doesn't directly say he enjoys sunbathing in the text, but he does use the words 'me encanta tumbarme al sol' which implies that he does. You may not recognise the verb *tumbarse*, but the fact that he's in the sun, by a pool and not doing anything else but reading suggests that he enjoys sunbathing.

Your turn!

Here is another exam-style question which requires you to put into practice the skills you have worked on, especially recognising and understanding words in relation to each other. ✎

Exam-style question

Holiday plans

Read Mariela's note below.

> **Por la mañana**
>
> Asistir a una clase de yoga antes de llevar el coche a arreglar. Ir a comprar un bañador nuevo y sandalias para el verano. Comprar un bocadillo y fruta para comer más tarde.
>
> **Por la tarde**
>
> Alquilar una bici para dar un paseo por el río. Visitar el museo después de comer en el parque. Después de devolver la bici, recoger el coche y pagar al mecánico.

When reading the text, look out for prepositions such as *por, para, de* and *a* which might indicate why someone is doing something.

Complete each sentence using a word from the box below. There are more words than gaps.

museum	supermarket	gym	bike hire	garage	clothes shop
river	park	restaurant	swimming pool	river	petrol station

Example: Before taking her car to be fixed Mariela goes to the ....gym............... .

(a) To be ready for her summer holiday Mariela needs to go

to the ....   (1)

(b) To buy her lunch she goes to the ....   (1)

(c) Before going cycling she goes to the ....   (1)

(d) After lunch she will go to the ....   (1)

(e) Finally, she has to go to the ....   (1)

(5 marks)

Read the parts of the question carefully, looking out for words like 'before', 'after' and 'finally', which signal where to find the information in the text.

Review your skills

Check up

Review your responses to the exam-style questions on pages 7 and 8. Tick ✓ the column that shows how well you think you have done each of the following.

	Not quite ✓	Nearly there ✓	Got it! ✓
recognised common words	☐	☐	☐
shown understanding of common words	☐	☐	☐
taken account of the context of common words	☐	☐	☐

Need more practice?

Go back to pages 2 and 3 and complete ✐ the two exam-style questions there. Use the checklist to help you.

Checklist In my answers, do I...	✓
identify and understand words from the topic lists?	
show that I've understood common words in my answer?	
use grammatical clues to work out my answer?	

Try to learn words in relation to each other. Group them into topics and then subgroup them again into topic areas (holidays: types of holiday, activities, weather, transport, places, accommodation, clothes, problems). You could make mind maps to help you remember the words.

How confident do you feel about each of these **skills**? Colour in ✐ the bars.

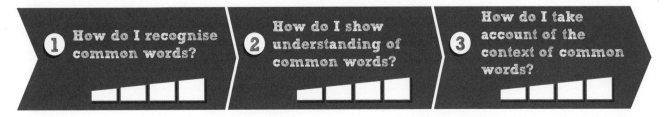

1. How do I recognise common words?

2. How do I show understanding of common words?

3. How do I take account of the context of common words?

② Recognising cognates and near-cognates

This unit will help you to learn how to use cognates and near-cognates so that you make sense of texts. The skills you will build are to:

- recognise and understand cognates (words that look and mean the same in both languages)
- recognise and understand near-cognates (words that look similar but whose forms or endings might be different)
- identify and be careful of 'false friends' (words that look the same or similar in both languages but mean something different).

In the exam, you will be asked to tackle reading tasks such as the ones below. This unit will prepare you to distinguish and understand different styles of texts, including magazine articles.

① Skim through the text below and underline Ⓐ the words that you can understand because they are cognates or near-cognates. Did you find any 'false friends'?

Do not answer this question yet. You will be asked to come back to it at the end of the unit.

Exam-style question

School problems

Read the article below.

> Un estudio del Ministerio de Educación sobre el acoso escolar concluye que la intimidación en las redes sociales representa uno de cada cuatro casos de acoso escolar en España. Sin embargo, a partir de los 13 años, el 36,5% de los casos de acoso son por ciberacoso. Otra conclusión es que el 70% de las víctimas de ciberacoso son chicas.
>
> El silencio ya no es una constante en los casos de acoso escolar. Ni por parte de las víctimas ni de sus compañeros. Más de la mitad de los estudiantes intimidados acusan a los agresores. Además, los profesores cada vez son más conscientes de lo que ocurre dentro y fuera del aula y en el patio.

Answer the following questions **in English**.

(a) How much bullying is done through social media?

.... (1)

(b) Who are the main victims of cyberbullying?

.... (1)

(c) Summarise how attitudes to bullying have changed.

.... (1)

(3 marks)

Understanding a text can sometimes hang on the meaning of one word in a sentence. If that word is a cognate or a near-cognate, it can help you. If it is a 'false friend', it can lead to errors, so beware!

Do not answer this question yet. You will be asked to come back to it at the end of the unit.

Exam-style question

My school

(a) Read Carmela's blog post about her school.

> Para mí, lo peor de mi instituto es que no hay instalaciones deportivas adecuadas como un gimnasio bien equipado. Como quiero estudiar ciencias deportivas en la universidad, esto es una frustración.
>
> Otro problema es que los laboratorios de ciencias son muy antiguos y por lo tanto no es fácil aprender en tales condiciones.

Answer the questions **in English**. You do not need to write full sentences.

(i) What is wrong with the sports facilities in Carmela's school?

.... (1)

(ii) What does she want to study at university?

.... (1)

(iii) Why isn't it easy to study science at her school?

.... (1)

(b) The blog continues.

> Lo bueno de mi insti son los profesores que son muy simpáticos, con la excepción del profesor de matemáticas, que es muy estricto. Mi profesora de español tiene muy buen humor y nos hace reír. Además, organiza excursiones extraescolares como visitas al cine a ver películas en español. De esa manera, nos divertimos aprendiendo.

(i) Who is strict at Carmela's school?

.... (1)

(ii) Where does the Spanish teacher sometimes take the students?

.... (1)

(5 marks)

The three key questions in the **skills boosts** will help you improve how you answer these types of questions.

 1 How do I recognise and understand cognates?

 2 How do I recognise and understand near-cognates?

 3 How do I identify and be careful of 'false friends'?

1 **How do I recognise and understand cognates?**

Many English and Spanish words have Latin or Greek roots and the same meaning; these words are called **cognates**. The Spanish language borrows many English words and vice versa. By knowing a few simple cognate rules, you can work out the meaning of many words.

When reading a text which might appear difficult at first, always look out for words that are the same or similar in both languages. This can help you make sense of the text.

1 Have a quick look at the three blog entries about school life. How do they seem to you at first glance? Tick ✓ a box.

very easy to understand ☐   fairly easy ☐   quite difficult ☐   very difficult ☐

A Voy al <u>club</u> de judo los jueves. En mi opinión, participar en las competiciones nacionales es una parte importante de la actividad. Además, en noviembre gané un trofeo.

B El uniforme en mi instituto es muy formal. Pienso que limita la individualidad, pero es práctico. Además, así las diferencias económicas entre los estudiantes no son tan obvias.

C Creo que las normas en el insti son necesarias. Por ejemplo, no se permite usar el móvil en clase y está prohibido ser agresivo o grosero. También hay que ser puntual.

2 Now read the three blog entries in **1** again and underline Ⓐ at least five words in each one that look the same or similar in English and mean the same in English.

3 **a** Read these sentences and highlight ✎ examples of words that demonstrate the spelling differences in the box below. The first word is done for you.

f	= ph	física	physics / physical
es	= s	especial	special
-ión	= -ion	televisión	television
i	= y (as a vowel)	bicicleta	bicycle

i   Esta es una foto de mis compañeros de la gimnasia.

ii   En la clase de geografía, estudiamos la contaminación y el reciclaje.

iii   Hicimos una excursión para ver el estadio de los Juegos Olímpicos.

iv   Gané un trofeo de esquí cuando fuimos a España.

v   Después de mucho estrés, aprobé el examen y me sentí fenomenal.

b On paper, write ✎ a list of these words with the English spelling alongside them and learn them.

2 How do I recognise and understand near-cognates?

There are thousands of words in Spanish which, although they are not exactly the same as in English, are easily understood if you are aware of some typical differences in spelling. These are known as near-cognates.

1 Practise recognising near-cognates. Read these sentences and note ✐ the number of cognates or near-cognates in each sentence in the box. Then write ✐ the English translations on paper.

a El profesor de educación de física es estricto y no tiene paciencia, pero controla bien la clase.
6

b Tengo que admitir que me gusta estudiar historia y geografía.

c La nota es para informar a mis padres que iré al club de fotografía mañana.

d Voy a decidir si participar en el concurso de teatro es buena idea o no.

e Desafortunadamente el uniforme de mi colegio en primaria era feo.

f Para hacer esta actividad es necesario poner atención y aprender el vocabulario.

g En mi insti no hay mucha intimidación ni violencia entre los estudiantes.

h Tengo la oportunidad de participar en un intercambio y visitar a mi amigo español.

i Estoy estudiando para el examen de biología. Tengo que escribir sobre un experimento.

j Mi compañero no es estúpido; es muy inteligente, pero es muy tímido.

2 Fill in ✐ the table with examples from the sentences above.

Spanish	English	Examples from sentences
English verbs ending in consonant, add -ar or -ir		controlar/control
-ar or -ir	-e	
Nouns or adjectives ending in -encia	-ence	
-ario	-ary	
-ción	-tion	
-dad	-ty	
-ía/-ia/-ío/-io	-y	
English nouns and adjectives ending in consonant, add -o/a or -e		
Adverbs ending in -mente	-ly	

3 Look for other changes between Spanish and English words in the sentences above and note ✐ them on paper.

Don't forget that Spanish cognates may have accents: rápido/rápidamente

③ How do I identify and be careful of 'false friends'?

If cognates and near-cognates are 'good friends', you need to be aware of 'false friends' – words which look identical or similar in both languages but have a different meaning (sometimes very different).

① Read the sentences in Spanish about school life. Then read the word-for-word translations. You'll soon notice they don't make sense! Underline Ⓐ the 'false friends' in the Spanish text and rewrite 🖉 the translations with words that make sense in the context, as in the example.

Example:

En el concurso de gimnasia no tuve <u>éxito</u> y salí en <u>último</u> lugar.

In the gymnastics competition I didn't have an exit and I came out in ultimate place.

In the gymnastics competition I wasn't successful and I came last.

ⓐ
Mi amigo es una persona sensible y le disgustan las discusiones en el patio.

My friend is a sensible person and he is disgusted by discussions on the patio.

ⓑ
La comida del insti es bastante sana, pero las sopas son saladas y por lo tanto siempre bebo un vaso de agua.

The food at school is quite sane but the soap is salad and therefore I always drink a vase of water.

ⓒ
Mi profesora envía cartas a casa si no somos educados.

My teacher envies letters home if we aren't educated.

ⓓ
No recuerdo dónde está la parada de autobús escolar.

I don't record where the parade of scholar bus is.

> Remember that word order in Spanish isn't always the same as in English. For example, adjectives follow nouns.

ⓔ
Voy a realizar una encuesta para ver cuántas personas asisten a los clubs extraescolares.

I'm going to realise a survey to see how many people assist in the extracurricular activities.

② Read the list of common 'false friends'. Find the correct English translations in the box and write them 🖉 down. Keep a note of any others you come across.

countryside/field	pay attention	to catch a cold	misfortune
at the moment	pregnant	meeting	to crash

ⓐ actual ....

ⓑ atender ....

ⓒ campo ....

ⓓ constiparse ....

ⓔ chocar ....

ⓕ una desgracia ....

ⓖ embarazada ....

ⓗ reunión ....

> The best way to avoid being fooled by 'false friends' is to keep a note of the most common ones and learn them.

Your turn!

Here is an exam-style question which you can use to practise the skills you have worked on, particularly how to use cognates and near-cognates to help you understand a text. 🖉

Exam-style question

After-school activities

(a) Read this blog about the school clubs Jorge goes to.

> Me gusta cambiar de clubs y actividades extraescolares cada trimestre porque me gusta aprender cosas nuevas. Esta vez seré miembro de la orquesta. Llevo dos años aprendiendo a tocar la trompeta y ya estoy listo para tocar con otras personas. Además, creo que participar en un concierto es algo muy gratificante.

Answer the following questions **in English**. You do not need to write full sentences.

(i) How often does Jorge change clubs?

.... **(1)**

(ii) How long has he been playing the trumpet?

.... **(1)**

(iii) What does he think he is ready for?

.... **(1)**

(b) The blog continues.

> Aparte de la música me chifla la natación. Nado los miércoles después del insti, cuando vamos a la piscina del polideportivo municipal. El instructor tiene mucha confianza en nosotros y participamos en concursos nacionales. Ganar un trofeo es mi sueño, pero el problema es que entrenar requiere mucho tiempo.

(i) Where is the swimming pool?

.... **(1)**

(ii) What is Jorge's dream?

.... **(1)**

(5 marks)

Make use of cognates or near-cognates to understand the text. Here, in the context of school clubs, *orquesta* is likely to mean exactly the same in English as in Spanish.

Be careful of 'false friends'! Remember, it's not always because a Spanish word looks similar to an English word that it means the same! Does *listo* mean the same in both languages?

Your turn!

Here is an exam-style question which you can use to practise the skills you have worked on, particularly recognising cognates and near-cognates and also spotting false friends, which can cause misunderstanding. 🖊

> Always be on the lookout for words that are going to help you make sense of the texts, such as cognates or near-cognates with their typical spelling changes. Also remember that some words despite sharing the same or similar spelling in both languages do not share the same meaning.

Exam-style question

My trip to Liverpool

Read Alfonso's blog about taking part in an exchange.

Hace poco estuve en Liverpool en un intercambio. Al principio, me disgustaba todo: el ritmo de vida, el hablar, los horarios para comer… Pero poco a poco empecé a acostumbrarme a las diferencias y por fin empecé a ver similitudes entre los dos países. Por ejemplo, la cosa que encontré más curiosa fue que los alumnos ingleses no pueden llevar su propia ropa. Sin embargo, en España también terminamos llevando el mismo uniforme: ¡vaqueros! Un intercambio es algo que recomiendo a cualquier estudiante de idiomas, no solo porque mejoras tus conocimientos del idioma, sino también porque aprendes mucho sobre la vida diaria y las costumbres de otro país y esto para mí fue lo más interesante.

Answer the following questions **in English**.

(a) How did Alfonso start to feel after a while?

.... (1)

(b) What did Alfonso find the most strange?

.... (1)

(c) Summarise why he thinks exchanges are a valuable experience.

.... (1)

(3 marks)

Review your skills

Check up

Review your responses to the exam-style questions on pages 15 and 16. Tick ✓ the column that shows how well you think you have done each of the following.

	Not quite ✓	Nearly there ✓	Got it! ✓
recognised and understood cognates	☐	☐	☐
recognised and understood near-cognates	☐	☐	☐
identified and been careful of 'false friends'	☐	☐	☐

Need more practice?

Go back to pages 10 and 11 and complete ✐ the two exam-style questions there. Use the checklist to help you.

Checklist In my answers, do I...	✓
check if there are any cognates in the text that can help me understand?	
locate words which I can easily understand if I adapt the spelling?	
notice if there are false friends I need to be careful of?	

Remember to use your common sense when deciding whether a Spanish word that looks like an English word means the same or not. You need to make sure it fits the context.

How confident do you feel about each of these **skills**? Colour in ✐ the bars.

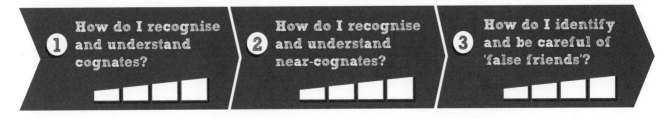

1. How do I recognise and understand cognates?

2. How do I recognise and understand near-cognates?

3. How do I identify and be careful of 'false friends'?

③ Synonyms and antonyms

This unit will help you to answer exam questions by identifying words with similar and opposite meanings and by working out the topic they belong to. The skills you will build are to:

- recognise words with similar meanings (synonyms)
- recognise words with opposite meanings (antonyms)
- identify words from the topic group they belong to.

In the exam, you will be asked to do reading tasks similar to the one below. This unit will prepare you to tackle these questions and choose or come up with the best answers.

① Look at the exam-style task below. Read the email. Does Marisa have a positive or negative view of her stay last year? Circle Ⓐ the words that helped you decide.

Do not answer this question yet. You will be asked to come back to it at the end of the unit.

Exam-style question

An exchange
Read Marisa's email below.

✉   — ☐ ✕

Hola Esteban.

Gracias por ayudarme a encontrar una familia inglesa para el intercambio. El año pasado estuve en un curso de verano y me quedé en casa de unos señores que eran bastante antipáticos, con niños traviesos y un perro muy desobediente. ¡No lo pasé bien!

Me gustaría estar en una familia más amable, que se lleva bien y con niños simpáticos de mi edad. Tengo 15 años y soy activa, positiva y sociable. Me encanta practicar deportes, sobre todo la natación, el ciclismo y el atletismo. Prefiero estar al aire libre que en casa, pero también puedo divertirme con un buen libro o una película.

Mil gracias y hasta pronto

Marisa

Complete the gaps in each sentence using a word from the box below. There are more words than gaps.

badly   behaved   reading   ~~family~~   fifteen   friend   funny   kind   sporty   talkative   unfriendly

Example: Marisa is looking for an English exchange _family_ .

(a) Last year she stayed with a family who were quite ....   **(1)**

(b) They had a dog and children who were ....   **(1)**

(c) This year, she would like to stay in a family with children who are about ....   **(1)**

(d) She describes herself as being outgoing and ....   **(1)**

(e) She says she's an outdoor person, but she also likes ....   **(1)**

                                                  (5 marks)

Do not answer this question yet. You will be asked to come back to it at the end of the unit.

Exam-style question

Manolito Gafotas by Elvira Lindo

Read the extract from the text. Manolito and his father have just been to the opticians.

> Después del oculista fuimos a desayunar a una cafetería. Yo le dije a mi padre que quería sentarme en un taburete de los de la barra, de esos que dan vueltas. Molaba tres kilos. Mi padre me dejó pedir un batido, una palmera de chocolate y un donuts. No había ningún otro niño en la cafetería. Me miré en el espejo de la cafetería para verme el peinado que me había hecho esa mañana y pensé: "A lo mejor creen que soy un niño, a lo mejor piensan que en vez de ocho años tengo dieciocho." […]
>
> El camarero se acercó a mi padre y le dijo:
>
> – Parece que el niño tiene hambre – luego me dijo a mí –: Como sigas comiendo así te vas a hacer más alto que tu papá. –

Put a cross [X] in the correct box.

Example: The story is taking place…

- [X] A in the morning.
- [ ] B in the afternoon.
- [ ] C in the evening.
- [ ] D at lunchtime.

(i) The boy and his father are sitting…

- [ ] A at a table inside.
- [ ] B at the bar.
- [ ] C at a table outside.
- [ ] D at home.

(ii) The boy has a…

- [ ] A coffee.
- [ ] B milkshake.
- [ ] C tea.
- [ ] D glass of water.

(iii) The boy has…

- [ ] A nothing to eat.
- [ ] B a packet of crisps.
- [ ] C an apple.
- [ ] D two sweet things.

(iv) In the café there are…

- [ ] A no other children.
- [ ] B several other children.
- [ ] C one other child.
- [ ] D two babies.

(v) The boy and his father are served by…

- [ ] A a woman.
- [ ] B a man.
- [ ] C a girl.
- [ ] D a young lady.

(5 marks)

The three key questions in the **skills boosts** will help you improve how you answer these types of questions.

 1 How do I recognise words with similar meanings (synonyms)?

 2 How do I recognise words with opposite meanings (antonyms)?

 3 How do I identify words from the topic group they belong to?

① **How do I recognise words with similar meanings (synonyms)?**

A **synonym** is a word that has the same meaning as another word. Some synonyms have the same roots, for example, *averiguar* and *verificar* from the Latin word 'veritas' (truth); they both mean 'to check that something is true'. But others don't look similar, even if they mean the same; for example, *acabar* and *terminar* (to finish).

Near-synonyms have meanings which are similar rather than the same; for example, *simpático – amable, honrado – honesto, todos los días – cada día, malo – travieso, pasearse – dar una vuelta.*

You may know more synonyms in Spanish than you think. The tasks on this page will help you to recognise and remember some of them.

① Write ✎ the words or phrases from the box that mean the same or nearly the same as the following:

Example: gratis   *gratuito*

a	tengo que	....
b	a menudo	....
c	fiel	....
d	desafortunadamente	....
e	usar	....
f	dar una vuelta	....
g	un e-mail	....
h	el ordenador	....
i	el teléfono	....
j	lo bueno de	....
k	se puede	....

> dar un paseo
> debo
> desgraciadamente
> el móvil
> el portátil
> es posible
> frecuentemente
> ~~gratuito~~
> la ventaja de
> leal
> un correo electrónico
> utilizar

② Read the sentences. Underline Ⓐ eight words or phrases that you can replace with synonyms from **①** and write ✎ them on the lines. Change the verb forms where necessary.

Example: La ventaja de la tecnología móvil es que siempre estás en contacto con los amigos.

　　　　Lo bueno de ....

a Se utilizan mucho las aplicaciones como WhatsApp e Instagram porque es gratuito mandar mensajes y fotos. ....

b Ahora se puede hacer casi todo en el teléfono, pero el portátil sirve mejor para hacer los deberes, ver vídeos y descargar música. ....

c Desgraciadamente, hay mucho fraude en Internet. ....

d Debes tener cuidado cuando recibes un correo electrónico de una empresa o una persona que no conoces. ....

2 **How do I recognise words with opposite meanings (antonyms)?**

Words with opposite meanings are called **antonyms**. Recognising them can help you to choose the correct answer for questions that don't use the same words as the text.

1 Sometimes antonyms are completely different words. Draw 🖉 lines to match the words into four pairs of antonyms:

A bien		a divertido
B aburrido		b menos
C distinto		c mal
D más		d parecido

You can recognise some antonyms by their **prefixes** (the letters at the start of a word):

simpático (nice, friendly)	**anti**pático (not nice, unfriendly)
afortunadamente (fortunately)	**des**afortunadamente (unfortunately)
posible (possible)	**im**posible (impossible)
soportable (bearable)	**in**soportable (unbearable)
responsable (responsible)	**irr**esponsable (irresponsible)

2 **a** Read the posts on a web forum about relationships with family and friends. On paper, write 🖉 the Spanish equivalents of the words in the box.

| talkative | we argue | optimistic | friendly | patient |

b Read the posts again and write 🖉 on paper the words that mean the opposite of the words from **a**.

Example: talkative <u>habladora</u> <u>callada</u>

Marina:	Mi hermana y yo somos gemelas, pero somos distintas de carácter: ella es bastante callada y yo soy muy habladora. Nos peleamos de vez en cuando, pero normalmente nos llevamos bien porque compartimos las mismas aficiones.
Juan:	Mi amigo José y yo nos conocemos desde la escuela primaria y creo que nos llevamos bien porque somos muy distintos. Él es optimista mientras yo suelo ser bastante pesimista.
Luisa:	Mi madre y yo nos peleamos siempre. Para ella soy 'imposible e inaguantable'. Dice que debo ser más responsable, pero creo que es ella quien tiene que ser menos impaciente.
Fernando:	Me divierto mucho con mi padre y casi nunca discutimos. Es muy serio y mucha gente piensa, al principio, que es antipático, pero cuando lo conocen, se dan cuenta de que es paciente, divertido y simpático.

---

3 Read the questions and write 🖉 the correct letter: M (Marina), J (Juan), L (Luisa) or F (Fernando). Use your answers to **2** to help you.

According to the posts on the web forum, who...

Example: gets on well with a sibling? <u>M</u>

a hardly ever argues with a parent? ....

b has a friend who is an optimist? ....

c is unbearable, according to their mother? ....

d has a father who is often thought to be unfriendly at first? ....

e gets on well with someone because they are different? ....

f gets on well with a family member because they have the same interests? ....

g thinks their mother should be more patient? ....

③ How do I identify words from the topic group they belong to?

Learning words in **topic groups** makes it easier to remember them. Recognising which topic group a word belongs to can help you to remember its meaning. Also, words from a particular topic group give you clues about the context of a reading text.

① **a** Read the texts. Select and write ✏️ the topic group from the box for each text.

> films   food   hometown and local area   leisure activities
> personality   physical description   weather

> Creo que las biografías son interesantes, pero las encuentro bastante serias. Me chiflan las novelas de ciencia ficción y también me encantan las historias de vampiros.

i ....

> Hoy, en el norte del país, hace mucho viento. En el este hace sol por la mañana, pero va a llover por la tarde.

ii ....

> Mi amiga Julia es muy guapa. Es alta y delgada. Tiene el pelo moreno, largo y ondulado. Tiene los ojos marrones.

iii ....

> De primer plato, tenemos ensalada de mariscos o gazpacho. De segundo, hay pollo a la brasa o gambas a la plancha. De postre, hay flan, helado o fruta.

iv ....

b Read the texts in **a** again and circle Ⓐ the words that fit the topic group you selected.

② **a** Read the texts and circle Ⓐ the correct topic (A or B).

> Este modelo es el más rápido con **una velocidad** máxima de 200 kilómetros por hora. Además, es el más lujoso y más cómodo de la nueva serie. Debajo de los asientos de detrás, hay **un cajón** especial para poner los portátiles, el monedero, los móviles o las cámaras.

i **A** home and contents   **B** transport and travel

> Acabamos de salir del estadio. ¡El partido fue fantástico! Vamos a coger un taxi porque está lloviendo y hay muchísima gente haciendo cola para entrar al metro – incluyendo **los hinchas** del otro equipo, ¡todos de mal humor por **la derrota**!

ii **A** sports and leisure   **B** climate and weather

b Underline Ⓐ the words or phrases that helped you choose the topic of each text.

③ You have identified the words that suggest the topic groups. Do the words you underlined in ② help you work out the meaning of the words in bold? Circle Ⓐ the correct answer.

a	**una velocidad**	a price	a size	a speed
b	**un cajón**	a seat	a box	a light
c	**los hinchas**	the supporters	the stadium staff	the groundsmen
d	**la derrota**	the victory	the defeat	the weather

Your turn!

Here is an exam-style question which you can use to practise the skills you have worked on, particularly how identifying the topic words belong to can help you understand the text.

① Look at the underlined words in each app description below. Write down ✏ a topic for each one.

Example: *En forma – sports and leisure*

Exam-style question

The best apps for...

Read the descriptions of these four apps.

— □ ✕

A   *En forma*

Esta aplicación sirve para cualquier actividad al aire libre: correr, andar o caminar. Le indica rutas y distancias recorridas, además del tiempo y las calorías usadas.

B   *Sabelotodo*

Tiene una base de datos donde puedes buscar las respuestas sobre ciencias, historia, matemáticas o geografía.

C   *Organízate*

La mejor manera de organizar los deberes o las tareas en casa, en el instituto o en la oficina. Se puede guardar qué tareas hay que hacer y las fechas para hacerlas.

D   *Lengua mundo*

Esta aplicación funciona en el móvil y en el ordenador. Cada lección tiene ejercicios para hablar, escuchar y traducir otros idiomas.

Choose the best app for each person. Enter **En forma**, **Sabelotodo**, **Organízate** or **Lengua mundo**.

You can use each app name more than once.

Example: I want to learn some Portuguese because I'm going to Brazil.   *Lengua mundo*

(a)   My son needs to plan his study time and not be late with homework.

....   (1)

(b)   It would be useful to measure how far and how fast I run.

....   (1)

(c)   My aunt wants to learn Chinese, but she hasn't got a smartphone.

....   (1)

(d)   My children ask me questions about homework that I can't answer.

....   (1)

(e)   I need to make a schedule for my exam revision.   ....   (1)

(f)   I would like to run a marathon next autumn.   ....   (1)

(6 marks)

Your turn!

Here is an exam-style question which you can use to practise the skills you have worked on, particularly how spotting synonyms and antonyms can help you to understand the text. ✍

> Look for words in the text that mean the same or are the opposite of these words:
>
> fiel   divertido   paciente   optimista   me gusta

Exam-style question

My friend Daniel

(a) Read this letter about friendship in an online magazine.

> Un buen amigo (o una buena amiga) tiene que ser leal; esto es lo más importante. Debe ayudarte cuando tienes problemas y apoyarte en todo. Siempre debe decirte la verdad. Tengo un amigo estupendo que se llama Daniel. Me divierto con él porque es muy gracioso y me hace reír. Nos llevamos muy bien y casi nunca discutimos.

Answer the following question **in English**. You do not need to write in full sentences.

According to the writer, ...

(i)   what is the most important quality of a best friend?

.... (1)

(ii) why does she have fun when she's with Daniel?

.... (1)

(b) The letter continues.

> Lo bueno de nuestra amistad es que somos muy distintos de carácter. Daniel es muy tranquilo y casi siempre está de buen humor mientras yo suelo ser impaciente, demasiado seria y bastante pesimista. Además, no compartimos las mismas aficiones: a él le encanta descargar y escuchar música rock a todo volumen y a mí no me gusta nada. A mí me chifla leer ciencia ficción y Daniel prefiere las historias de vampiros.

(i)   According to the writer, what is the advantage of her friendship with Daniel?

.... (1)

(ii) Who would you say is more optimistic, Daniel or the writer?

.... (1)

(iii) How do their tastes in music and books differ?

.... (1)

(5 marks)

Review your skills

Check up

Review your responses to the exam-style questions on pages 23 and 24. Tick ✓ the column that shows how well you think you have done each of the following.

	Not quite ✓	Nearly there ✓	Got it! ✓
recognised words with similar meanings	☐	☐	☐
recognised words with opposite meanings	☐	☐	☐
identified words from the topic they belong to	☐	☐	☐

Need more practice?

Go back to pages 18 and 19 and complete ✎ the two exam-style questions there. Use the checklist to help you.

Checklist In my answers, do I...	✓
look for words I know to give me an idea of the context?	
notice words with similar and opposite meanings?	
identify words with opposite meanings by their prefix?	
recognise words I know from a particular topic group to help me understand unfamiliar words?	

Remember that in both literary texts and other exam texts there will always be words you don't know. Do not focus on these. Always start by looking for words and phrases you *do* know. They will help you to get an idea of what the text is about and, in turn, this will help you with the vocabulary you do not know.

How confident do you feel about each of these **skills**? Colour in ✎ the bars.

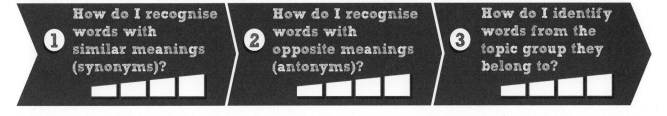

1. How do I recognise words with similar meanings (synonyms)?

2. How do I recognise words with opposite meanings (antonyms)?

3. How do I identify words from the topic group they belong to?

Identifying relevant information

This unit will help you to learn how to make sure you identify the information needed to answer a question. The skills you will build are to:

- make sure you understand question words
- locate answers in a text
- deal with unfamiliar words.

In the exam, you will be asked to do reading tasks similar to the one below. This unit will prepare you to tackle these questions and choose or come up with the best answers.

1. In this exam-style question, the article includes several questions. Can you find five question words? (**Clue**: they all have accents and an upside-down question mark '¿' before them.) Highlight 🖉 the question words and write 🖉 what they mean in English on paper.

Do not answer this question yet. You will be asked to come back to it at the end of the unit.

Exam-style question

Look at the title of the article to find out what it's about. If you don't know what all the words mean, focus on the words you do know.

La juventud española y el tiempo libre

Lee este artículo sobre el tiempo libre.

> ¿Con quién prefieren pasar sus ratos libres los jóvenes españoles y qué suelen hacer? La mayoría dice que le gusta estar con los amigos y los pasatiempos mencionados más a menudo son dar una vuelta, ir al cine o ir de excursión. ¿Cómo contactan con sus amigos y compañeros para salir? Pues, con el móvil; esto sí es la respuesta de todos.
>
> ¿Cuáles son sus deportes preferidos? El fútbol, desde luego, sobre todo entre los chicos, pero ahora hay cada vez más equipos femeninos. Se practican también el baloncesto, la natación y el ciclismo.
>
> ¿Dónde pasan la mayoría de sus horas libres los jóvenes? En casa, para estudiar, leer, escuchar música, ver deportes y películas, y para descansar.

Completa cada frase con una palabra del recuadro de abajo. No necesitas todas las palabras.

| casa | ~~amigos~~ | chicas | familia | móvil | caballo | cine | paseo | bicicleta |
| ordenador | atletas | padres | | | | | | |

Ejemplo: Los jóvenes prefieren pasar el tiempo con los   _amigos_   .

(a) Una actividad frecuente es ir de ....   (1)

(b) Para quedar con los amigos, los jóvenes usan el ....   (1)

(c) Ahora juegan más al fútbol las ....   (1)

(d) Otros deportes preferidos son nadar y montar en ....   (1)

(e) Aunque los jóvenes españoles son sociables y activos, también
les gusta estar en ....   (1)

(5 marks)

2 You need to look for information in each section of the text to match to the sentences a–e below. Write which comment (a)–(e) below matches the information in the first paragraph of the text. ....

Do not answer this question yet. You will be asked to come back to it at the end of the unit.

Exam-style question

Telediario

Lee esta información sobre los programas de televisión.

> **Cocineros de primera**
>
> Los concursantes compiten para ser el mejor de todos. Esta semana, tienen que aprovechar al máximo los productos de la región.
>
> **La vida de los animales**
>
> Conocemos los secretos de los desiertos y los grandes espacios abiertos en África y en Sudamérica.
>
> **Diario deportivo**
>
> Fórmula 1, Gran Premio en el circuito de Cataluña y MotoGP desde Holanda. A ver quiénes se ponen a la cabeza de los campeonatos.
>
> **Gran Hermano**
>
> Acaban de entrar en la casa los nuevos habitantes que vivirán juntos durante las próximas semanas. Las cámaras los filmarán 24 horas al día.

¿Cuál es el programa ideal para cada persona? Escoge entre **Cocineros de primera, La vida de los animales, Diario deportivo** o **Gran Hermano**. Puedes usar los nombres de los programas más de una vez.

Ejemplo: Me gustan los documentales.   *La vida de los animales* ....

(a) Las carreras de coches son muy emocionantes. .... (1)

(b) Soy adicto a los *reality*. .... (1)

(c) Me encantan los programas informativos sobre la naturaleza. .... (1)

(d) Veo todos los programas sobre comida y cocina. .... (1)

(e) Me gustan todos los deportes desde el fútbol hasta el automovilismo.

.... (1)

(5 marks)

The three key questions in the **skills boosts** will help you improve how you answer these types of questions.

1 How do I make sure I understand question words?

2 How do I locate answers in a text?

3 How do I deal with unfamiliar words?

1 **How do I make sure I understand question words?**

For some exam tasks, you will answer questions in English, so look carefully at the question words and make sure you find the exact information in the Spanish text. Also, make sure you understand the question words in Spanish within the Spanish texts and instructions.

① Write ✏ the correct English question word beside each Spanish word.

who	what	where	when	why	which	how	how much

a qué ....

b quién ....

c cuándo ....

d dónde ....

e cuánto ....

f cómo ....

g cuál ....

h por qué ....

> The question words *quién, cuánto* and *cuál* are adjectives in some questions and need to agree with the noun they refer to. For example: ¿**Quiénes** fueron al cine? ¿**Cuántas** horas al día trabajas? ¿**Cuáles** son tus libros preferidos?

② Read the questions focusing on the question words. What does each one tell you about the information it is asking for? Choose an idea for each one. Write ✏ it beside the question.

a number	a person	~~a place~~	a reason	a time	an activity	a choice

a ¿Dónde viven tus abuelos? *a place* ....

b ¿Cuáles son los regalos más adecuados para tus padres, un libro y un CD o dos entradas para un concierto? ....

c ¿Quién es tu modelo a seguir? ....

d ¿Por qué admiras a esta persona? ....

e ¿Cúantas veces has visto tu película favorita? ....

f ¿Cuándo estudias mejor, por la mañana o por la tarde? ....

g ¿Qué quieres hacer este fin de semana? ....

③ Match each of the following answers to the correct question in **②** and write ✏ the letters below. Use the idea you wrote beside each question to help you.

a Las entradas, porque les encanta la música. ....

b ¡Cinco creo, o quizás más! ....

c En Sudamérica, por eso no los veo muy a menudo. ....

d Por la tarde, porque por la mañana soy muy dormilón. ....

e Ir al cine con mis amigos. ....

f Mi hermano mayor. ....

g Porque es inteligente, trabajador y simpático. ....

② How do I locate answers in a text?

In most tasks, the information in the text is in the same order as the questions. Start by reading the text. Next, read through the questions. Then look at each question in turn and find the answer for each one as you read through the text again.

① Read the text and questions. What information does each one ask you to find? Underline (A) the key words in each question, then highlight (✎) the word or words in the text that give you the key information and write (✎) the letter of the question next to it.

> **Natalia Tena, actriz y cantante**
>
> Natalia Tena es actriz y cantante ^*a*^ . Nació en Londres en 1984 y es de nacionalidad británica. Habla inglés y español porque sus padres son de España. Además habla vasco, el idioma del País Vasco, que es la región del norte de España de donde proviene su padre.
>
> Natalia es la cantante del grupo Molotov Jukebox y también toca el acordeón. Como actriz, ha salido en las películas de Harry Potter y en la serie de televisión *Juego de tronos*.

a What kind of <u>work</u> does Natalia Tena do?　　**d** Which part of Spain is her father from?

b Where is she from?　　**e** Which instrument does Natalia play?

c How many languages does she speak?　　**f** Which TV series has she appeared in?

② Now write (✎) the answers to the questions in ① in English on paper.

③ Read what four Spanish teenagers have posted about their free time. Look at each of the descriptions a–f below. Find and highlight (✎) the words in the posts that match the descriptions. Write (✎) the names in the spaces.

> 💬　　　　　　　　　　　　　　　　　　　　　　　　— ☐ ✕
>
> Lo que más me gusta es salir con mis amigos a dar una vuelta, a charlar y pasar el rato.
> 　　　　　　　　　　　　　　　　　　　　　　　　　Lorena
>
> Toco el teclado y me encanta escuchar todo tipo de música, especialmente la electrónica.
> 　　　　　　　　　　　　　　　　　　　　　　　　　Carlos
>
> Me gusta el deporte. Juego al fútbol y al voleibol. ¡Me gusta ganar!
> 　　　　　　　　　　　　　　　　　　　　　　　　　Nina
>
> No soy teleadicto, pero para descansar, me encanta ver comedias y series policíacas.
> 　　　　　　　　　　　　　　　　　　　　　　　　　Manolo

Who does each sentence describe? **Lorena, Carlos, Nina** or **Manolo**?

a .... is active and sporty.　　**d** .... plays and listens to music.

b .... relaxes by watching TV.　　**e** .... likes comedies and crime series.

c ...*Lorena*............ is <u>friendly</u> and <u>sociable</u>.　　**f** .... is competitive.

> With this type of question, the answers are not in the order of the texts, so you need to use the key words in the descriptions to help you locate the answers.

Skills boost

> ### 3 How do I deal with unfamiliar words?

You can deal with a word you don't know by looking at its context. Look at the rest of the phrase or the sentence and try to work out the meaning.

(1) (a) Read these six extracts from a music festival website. You might not know the words in bold. Circle (A) the words you know that can help you work out the meaning of the words in bold. Look at the example to help you.

> *is ideal for*   *because there is great music*
>
> **Example:** Este festival (es ideal para) los más **melómanos** (porque hay música fantástica) y muy variada.

  i La lista de los grupos está en los **carteles** que puedes ver en los sitios públicos y en Internet.

  ii El festival **tiene lugar** del 27 al 29 de abril.

  iii La entrada cuesta 65 euros con zona de **acampada** incluida para dormir.

  iv Si no quieres llevar tu propia **tienda**, la organización te la alquila por pocos euros.

  v Este año **encabezan** Los Locos y Kaos Urbano y hay más de 140 grupos en total.

(b) Now underline (A) the correct option for each word.

> **Example: melómanos**   football fans / <u>music lovers</u> / dance fans

  i **carteles**   tickets / menus / posters

  ii **tiene lugar**   takes place / is on sale / is sold out

  iii **acampada**   cooking / showers / camping

  iv **tienda**   shop / tent / sun hat

  v encabezan   aren't playing / are supporting / are headlining

- You can also look for cognates and near-cognates (words that are similar in English and Spanish). For example, *acampada* is similar to 'camping'.
- To understand a word like *encabezan* you can see a Spanish word within it that you know: *cabeza* = 'head'.

(2) Read the comments about films, books and TV series. Which word from the box would you expect to find in the gap in each sentence? Then fill in (✏️) the gaps with the correct words.

> decepcionado (disappointed)   emocionante (exciting)
> escalofriante (frightening, chilling)   impresionante (impressive)

> Remember to make the adjectives agree where necessary.

(a) Prefiero las películas de acción y de aventuras porque son más

.... que las comedias y las pelis de amor.

(b) Juan, creo que te quedaste bastante .... con el último episodio de la serie. No era tan bueno como los otros, ¿verdad?

(c) Anoche fuimos al cine y vimos una película de terror. ¡Qué miedo! Era

....

(d) La última novela de Ruiz Zafón es .... por los originales personajes que se presentan y por el estilo ágil de la narración.

(3) Circle (A) the words in the sentences in **(2)** that helped you choose the correct missing word and write (✏️) the reason for your choice on paper. Look at the example to help you.

(a) *Action and adventure films are likely to be 'exciting.'*

Your turn!

Here is an exam-style question for you to practise the skills you have worked on, specifically how to deal with unfamiliar words.

Exam-style question

Guide to summer activities

Read an extract from a leaflet about summer activities.

A Gimcana acuática: juegos y concursos dentro y fuera del agua

¿Dónde?	En la playa
¿Cuándo?	De lunes a viernes, de las 10.30 a las 12.00
¿Para quién?	Niños a partir de los 4 años (imprescindible saber nadar)
¿Cuánto?	Gratuita

B Visita al museo romano

¿Dónde?	San Martí d'Empuries
¿Cuándo?	De las 10.00 a las 18.00 (cerrado los lunes)
¿Cuánto?	5 euros (3 euros mayores de 65 años; menores de 8 años entrada gratuita)

> You should use the context to work out the meaning of *imprescindible*. Also, use logic and your powers of deduction: it's a water activity so being able to swim is essential.

Complete the gap in each sentence using a word from the box below. There are more words than gaps.

five	afternoon	four	beach	free	morning	Sundays	5 euros	swim
Mondays	run	~~water~~						

Example: The games and competitions are on the beach and in the __water__.

(a) They take place every weekday ....   (1)

(b) To do this activity, children need to be at least ....   (1)

(c) Participants must be able to ....   (1)

(d) The Roman museum at San Martí d'Empuries is closed on ....   (1)

(e) Children under 8 years old can go in for ....   (1)

(5 marks)

Your turn!

Here is an exam-style question for you to practise the skills you have worked on, specifically how to locate information in a text. 🖊

Exam-style question

Sport and young people

Read the article below.

> ¿Qué tiene que ver el deporte con la salud?
>
> Los jóvenes que practican deporte tendrán menos problemas de salud en su futuro como adultos.
>
> ¿Cuánto tiempo deben dedicar al deporte los jóvenes?
>
> Se recomienda entre 30 minutos y una hora al día.
>
> ¿Cuáles son las ventajas del deporte?
>
> Se aconseja practicar deportes desde la niñez para evitar problemas como la obesidad y la depresión. Además, las actividades deportivas ayudan a los adolescentes a ser más disciplinados y constantes. Aprenden a trabajar en equipo y a respetar las reglas y al rival.

Answer the following questions **in English**.

(a) What is the long-term benefit of doing sport from a young age?

.... (1)

(b) How much exercise should a young person do on a daily basis?

.... (1)

(c) Summarise the benefits of doing sport from childhood.

.... (1)

(3 marks)

Look for cognates and near-cognates in the text to help you understand unfamiliar words. Look at Unit 2, pp 12–14 for more information.

Notice how the question words in the text match the questions in the task. They will help you find the answers.

Review your skills

Check up

Review your responses to the exam-style questions on pages 31 and 32. Tick ✓ the column that shows how well you think you have done each of the following.

	Not quite ✓	Nearly there ✓	Got it! ✓
made sure I understood question words	☐	☐	☐
located answers in a text	☐	☐	☐
dealt with unfamiliar words	☐	☐	☐

Need more practice?

Go back to pages 26 and 27 and complete ✐ the two exam-style questions there. Use the checklist to help you.

Never rush to write or fill in the answers! Read through the texts as many times as you need to so that you find the information the questions are asking.

Checklist In my answers, do I...	✓
read each text to get the gist of what it is about?	
then look carefully for the answer to each question?	
understand the question words where relevant?	
use the context to help me understand unfamiliar words?	
use logic, deduction and other clues to help me understand unfamiliar words?	
use other related Spanish words I know to help me understand unfamiliar words?	

How confident do you feel about each of these **skills**? Colour in ✐ the bars.

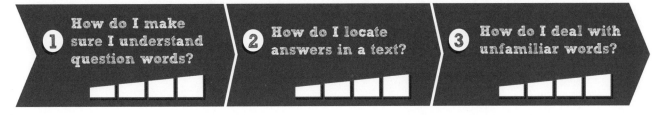

① How do I make sure I understand question words?

② How do I locate answers in a text?

③ How do I deal with unfamiliar words?

⑤ Using grammatical clues

This unit will help you use grammar to understand a text. The skills you will build are to:

- identify the way words relate to each other in a sentence
- make use of tenses to clarify meaning
- make use of pronouns to clarify meaning.

In the exam, you will be asked to tackle reading tasks such as the ones below. This unit will prepare you to write your response to these questions.

Do not answer this question yet. You will be asked to come back to it at the end of the unit.

Exam-style question

El doctor Centeno by Benito Pérez Galdós

Read the text about Felipe, a poor student, who is out with his boss, Alejandro.

> Eran las nueve y cuarto.
>
> Aunque era domingo, muchas tiendas estaban abiertas. Pasaron por una zapatería, cuyo iluminado escaparate contenía variedad de calzado* para ambos sexos.
>
> —Para, cochero* –gritó Alejandro–. Y tú, Felipe, baja. Te voy a comprar unas botas. […] Felipe bajó gozoso; entró en la tienda. Al poco rato volvió a decir a su amo*:
>
> —Me he puesto unas… Pide cincuenta y seis reales*.
>
> —Toma el dinero, paga y ven al momento.
>
> Al poco rato volvió a aparecer el gran Felipe llevando las botas nuevas y con las viejas en la mano.
>
> —¿Qué hago con éstas?
>
> —Tira eso, tíralas…
>
> Felipe las tiró en medio de la calle, no sin cierto desconsuelo porque las botas, aunque feas, todavía servían, […] y no le gustaba tirar cosa alguna.

In a literary text, remember that dashes at the start of lines indicate a dialogue.

If you are not sure you have understood enough to answer a question, check you are clear about the pronouns (subject pronouns, reflexive pronouns, object pronouns, etc.) and about the tense of the key verbs.

* *calzado = footwear*
* *cochero = driver*
* *amo = boss*
* *reales = old Spanish coin*

Answer the following questions **in English**. You do not need to write in full sentences.

(a) What day of the week was it when Felipe and Alejandro were out?

.... (1)

(b) Who paid for Felipe's new boots?

.... (1)

(c) Where did Felipe throw his old boots?

.... (1)

(d) Why was Felipe not happy to do what Alejandro asked him to do?

.... (1)

(4 marks)

Do not answer this question yet. You will be asked to come back to it at the end of the unit.

Exam-style question

Un pueblo en verano

Lee el blog de Marina.

Para ir al pueblo de mis abuelos tengo que tomar un tren a Madrid y después un autobús a un pueblo cercano. Desde allí tomo un taxi.

En el pueblo no hay tienda, pero todos los días viene el panadero y le compramos pan. Si queremos comprar más, vamos al supermercado en otro pueblo.

Lo mejor es que hay una piscina donde paso muchas tardes con mis primos.

No estuve para la fiesta del pueblo este verano porque fui a la costa. Pero el año pasado hubo una carrera de bicicleta y por la noche tocaron varias bandas en la plaza.

Pon una cruz [X] en la casilla correcta.

Ejemplo: Los abuelos de Marina son de…

- [X] A un pueblo rural.
- [ ] B Barcelona.
- [ ] C Madrid.
- [ ] D la costa.

(i) Para llegar al pueblo hay que tomar…

- [ ] A un tren.
- [ ] B un autobús.
- [ ] C un taxi.
- [ ] D varios medios de transporte.

(ii) La familia de Marina compra el pan…

- [ ] A en la tienda.
- [ ] B del panadero.
- [ ] C en el mercado.
- [ ] D en el supermercado.

(iii) A Marina le encanta…

- [ ] A el mercado.
- [ ] B la piscina.
- [ ] C la playa.
- [ ] D el campo.

(iv) Marina va a la piscina con sus…

- [ ] A primos.
- [ ] B abuelos.
- [ ] C amigos.
- [ ] D padres.

(v) Este año Marina fue a…

- [ ] A la fiesta del pueblo.
- [ ] B una carrera deportiva.
- [ ] C la playa.
- [ ] D un concierto de música.

(5 marks)

If you are not sure about what some parts of the text mean, analyse the sentences and identify the verb(s), the subject(s), or description(s). What tense is the main verb in?

The three key questions in the **skills boosts** will help you improve how you answer these types of questions.

1 How do I identify the way words relate to each other in a sentence?

2 How do I make use of tenses to clarify meaning?

3 How do I make use of pronouns to clarify meaning?

1 How do I identify the way words relate to each other in a sentence?

To help you make sense of a sentence, start from what you know. Look for the verb and then identify:
- the subject (who or what does the action): a noun, a pronoun or shown as part of the verb
- the object (who or what receives the action of the verb)
- the complement (any part of the sentence that gives you more information about the subject or the object).

① Read the sentences and identify the subject by circling Ⓐ the correct option for each underlined verb. Remember that in Spanish verbs don't always need to use pronouns to make their subject clear. Use the verb endings to help you.

Example: A veces ⌐yo⌐ / Cristina <u>voy</u> al centro comercial con mi hermana Cristina.

a Generalmente *Cristina / Cristina y yo* <u>compramos</u> ropa, aunque *Cristina / yo* <u>prefiero</u> comprar por Internet.

b Si <u>estoy</u> *Rafa y Tomás / yo* en el centro con mis amigos, siempre *Rafa y Tomás / yo* <u>quieren</u> comer algo.

c *Yo / Rafa, Tomás y yo* <u>vamos</u> a uno de los muchos restaurantes.

d Una vez *Rafa / Rafa, Tomás y yo* <u>fuimos</u> a un restaurante turco.

e La comida era deliciosa y *(Rafa y Tomás) / (la comida)* no <u>costaba</u> demasiado.

f La próxima vez *Rafa y Tomás / yo* <u>probarán</u> otro lugar.

② Read the texts and underline Ⓐ the information in each sentence that helps you choose the correct answer ✓. On paper, write ✎ a reason for your choice, as in the example.

Ejemplo:

> Aurora: Hoy es domingo y estoy en casa, pero el viernes juego al tenis y <u>voy al centro comercial el sábado.</u>

Aurora va de compras…

☐ **A** el viernes.   ✓ **B** el sábado.   ☐ **C** el domingo.   ☐ **D** el lunes.

key verb 'ir': 'voy' (verb first person singular), 'centro comercial' (complement – where you go shopping), 'el sábado' (when she goes shopping – correct answer)

a
> Mi amiga sólo compró un monedero, pero yo compré un vestido bastante caro.

Check the verb endings (-ó/-é) to find out who bought what.

Aurora compró…

☐ **A** un regalo.   ☐ **B** un monedero.   ☐ **C** ropa.   ☐ **D** un recuerdo.

b
> Prefiero los grandes almacenes a los centros comerciales porque todo está en un edificio.

Look at the word order. In this case check what Aurora likes by looking at the object immediately after the verb *preferir*.

A Aurora le gustan…

☐ **A** los grandes almacenes.   ☐ **C** las tiendas.
☐ **B** los centros comerciales.   ☐ **D** los edificios.

c
> Siempre voy de compras a las tiendas o el centro comercial, pero mi madre compra todo por Internet.

Check the verb endings. Here find what Aurora's mum does by looking for the third person singular of a verb (*compra*).

La madre de Aurora siempre hace sus compras…

☐ **A** en las tiendas.   ☐ **C** en el centro comercial.
☐ **B** en el supermercado.   ☐ **D** en línea.

2 **How do I make use of tenses to clarify meaning?**

The literary texts you have to read in the exam often combine verbs in the present tense, past tenses and the future tense.

• Recognise the forms of different tenses by learning common verb patterns.

• Understand when the two main past tenses, preterite and imperfect, are used.

1 **a** Look at the literary extract and the questions below. Write ✎ the tense you need to look for to find the answer in each case.

b Underline Ⓐ all the verbs in that tense in the extract.

c Use the tenses to help you answer ✎ the questions.

> Check you know the verb endings for the preterite, imperfect and future tenses.

***El libro de los cuentos* by Rafael Boira**

Las tiendas abiertas

Una amiga nuestra <u>solía</u> decir:

— Están tan frías las tiendas que tienes que llevar un abrigo para ir de compras. La última vez que fui cogí un constipado, pero no puedo resistir entrar en ellas porque están siempre abiertas.

— Pues buen remedio, un amigo le contestó. Debes ir sólo los días de fiesta por la tarde y las encontrarás cerradas.

Example: Who used to complain about the shops? <u>(3rd person singular, imperfect)</u> <u>A friend of ours</u>

i What is the woman's complaint about the shops? ....

ii Why can't the woman resist going in the shops? ....

iii What will the woman find if she goes shopping on public holidays? ....

2 **a** These short texts use both the imperfect and preterite tenses. Read the sentences and questions and underline Ⓐ the imperfect verbs and highlight ✎ the preterite verbs.

b Write down ✎ what tense you are looking for to find the answer to the question.

c Answer the questions. Mark the relevant box with a cross Ⓧ.

> Por la mañana mis padres y yo nos <u>bañábamos</u> en la playa, pero una tarde visitamos la capital.

Example: Un día Simona fue a…

   ☒ **A** la ciudad. ☐ **B** la playa. ☐ **C** nadar. ☐ **D** tomar el sol. *preterite*

> Hacía buen tiempo todos los días, pero una noche hubo una tormenta que nos sorprendió.

i Generalmente…

   ☐ **A** llovía. ☐ **B** hacía mal tiempo. ☐ **C** hacía sol. ☐ **D** nevaba. ....

> Un día comimos en un restaurante italiano, pero yo prefería comer bocadillos en la playa.

ii A Simona le gustaba comer…

   ☐ **A** en un restaurante. ☐ **B** en casa. ☐ **C** en una pizzería. ☐ **D** al aire libre.

....

3 How do I make use of pronouns to clarify meaning?

Pronouns replace nouns. Learn to recognise the most common ones.

Don't confuse reflexive pronouns with object pronouns, which usually appear in front of the verb as well.

Direct object pronouns replace something or someone that has already been mentioned. Some direct object pronouns have to agree with the noun they are replacing: *me, te, lo/la, nos, os, los/las.*	Indirect object pronouns are used to say 'to me', 'for him', etc. They are the same as direct object pronouns, but *lo/la* changes to *le* and *los/las* changes to *les.*
*Me gusta <u>esta falda</u>. Me **la** llevo.*	*¿Qué **me** recomienda?*
I like <u>this skirt</u>. I'll take **it**.	What do you recommend for **me**?

Note: If the verb is in the infinitive or imperative, the object pronoun is attached to the end of the verb: *Voy a comprar un cuaderno. Voy a comprar**lo**.* = I'm going to buy it.

*Ponte la chaqueta. Pónte**la**.* = Put it on.

① José talks about a shopping trip. Use the table above to circle Ⓐ the correct pronoun each time.

Quise comprar unas botas nuevas para el invierno. La zapatería estaba en la calle principal, pero no <u>lo</u> / <u>la</u> encontraba. Pedí direcciones a un hombre y <u>me</u> / <u>le</u> contestó: 'No <u>lo</u> / <u>la</u> encontrarás abierta, mejor ir a los grandes almacenes.' Tomé un autobús que <u>nos</u> / <u>me</u> llevó allí. Una dependienta <u>me</u> / <u>los</u> preguntó qué quería. <u>La</u> / <u>Le</u> contesté que quería unas botas. 'No <u>las</u> / <u>los</u> tenemos ahora porque es verano,' <u>le</u> / <u>me</u> contestó. '¿Qué <u>me</u> / <u>os</u> recomienda?' <u>le</u> / <u>la</u> pregunté. Al final, <u>me</u> / <u>la</u> compré unas sandalias.

② These sentences have been rewritten with pronouns replacing all or some of the nouns. For each sentence, underline Ⓐ the version that follows which conveys the same meaning. Watch out for changes in word order.

Ejemplo:

> Pilar ve a su padre, pero no ve a sus hermanos.

Pilar las ve, pero no lo ve a él. / <u>Pilar lo ve, pero no los ve a ellos.</u>

> Pronouns can help you find the right answer, but mistaking the meaning of a pronoun can lead you to answer incorrectly.

ⓐ Roberto da el dinero a Aurora y yo doy la entrada a Roberto.

Yo le doy el dinero y él la da la entrada. / Yo le doy la entrada y él le da el dinero.

ⓑ Lola y Pepa buscan recuerdos y Martín compra un juego.

Ellas le buscan y él los compra. / Ellas los buscan y él lo compra.

ⓒ Diana y yo apreciamos el campo, pero a Valentina y Lidia les gusta más.

Ellas lo aprecian y a nosotras nos gusta más. / Nosotras lo apreciamos, pero a ellas les gusta más.

ⓓ El señor dio el mapa a Pepe y Carlos, pero Pepe y Carlos no miraron el mapa.

Él se lo dio, pero ellos no lo miraron. / Ellos le miraron y él no se lo dio.

Your turn!

Here is an exam-style question which requires you to put into practice the skills you have worked on, specifically how to use understanding of tenses and pronouns to make sense of a text. 🖉

> To help you make sense of the narrative, remember that the preterite tense is used for completed actions in the past and the imperfect for describing what something was like as well as repeated actions.

> Use your knowledge of pronouns to help you answer the questions. Who does *le* refer to in the phrase *para llevarle a mi padre unos documentos*? Remember the rules about the position of pronouns on page 37.

Exam-style question

Entre la bruma by **Antonio Domínguez Hidalgo**

Read the text about Antonio travelling across the city to do something for his father.

> Tenía que ir hasta el otro lado de la ciudad para llevarle a mi padre unos documentos muy importantes. Sólo de pensar en lo aburrido y largo de la ruta, sentía un disgusto tremendo… ¡Por qué estaba tan lejos la oficina! En el sol de mediodía esperé el autobús cerca de veinte minutos. Al fin llegó, pero venía lleno… Subí al vehículo y parecía un horno y una caja de malos olores. Iba de pie rodando como una pelota.
>
> Me sentí mal por no estar haciendo lo que yo consideraba más útil: escuchar música, leer, estudiar, o conversar con mis amigos… hasta que al fin llegué a mi destino. Cumplí con las órdenes y desde allá vine a casa a pie… Era mejor caminar entre las tiendas, las calles estrechas y amplias, los edificios antiguos o modernos… Llegué a casa cerca de las once de la noche…

Answer the following questions **in English**. You do not need to write in full sentences.

> An authentic text like this one can be harder to understand. Once you have enough clues to answer the four questions, you can ignore the rest of the text.

(a) What was Antonio taking to his father?

.... (1)

(b) How did he travel there?

.... (1)

(c) What would he rather have been doing? Mention **one** thing.

.... (1)

(d) How did he get home?

.... (1)

(**4 marks**)

Your turn!

This is another exam-style question which requires you to put into practice the skills you have worked on, specifically using grammar clues to find information in a text. 🖉

- Analyse the sentences you are not sure about and identify the verb(s), the subject(s), the complement(s) or description(s). What tense is the main verb in?
- Use the pronouns as clues to the meaning. For example, who does the pronoun in *para él* refer to?
- Use grammar clues to help you in tasks like the one below.

Exam-style question

En el mercado del Rastro

Lee este artículo.

Para Marcos, el mejor lugar para pasar la mañana los domingos en Madrid era el mercado del Rastro. Iba a hacer fotos, tomarse un café o encontrarse con amigos. Pero lo mejor para él era comprar cosas raras.

Iba al Rastro en metro porque es imposible aparcar. Siempre llegaba para las diez, ya que más tarde habría demasiada gente.

El mercado no es por una sola calle sino por muchas y en ellas encontrarás puestos con ropa, zapatos, alimentos, artesanía, antigüedades… Una vez Marcos compró unos pendientes muy bonitos y se los regaló a una amiga. ¡Más tarde descubrieron que eran muy antiguos y valiosos!

Pon una cruz [X] en la casilla correcta.

Example: Marcos va al mercado…

- ☐ A todas las mañanas.
- ☒ B los domingos.
- ☐ C todos los días.
- ☐ D los fines de semana.

(i) A Marcos lo que le gustaba más del mercado era…

- ☐ A sacar fotos.
- ☐ B desayunar.
- ☐ C ver a amigos.
- ☐ D adquirir objetos.

(ii) Marcos viajaba al Rastro…

- ☐ A a pie.
- ☐ B en taxi.
- ☐ C en transporte público.
- ☐ D en coche.

(iii) Es preferible llegar cuando…

- ☐ A hay mucha gente.
- ☐ B hay menos gente.
- ☐ C no hay nadie.
- ☐ D es mediodía.

(iv) El mercado se extiende por…

- ☐ A una calle.
- ☐ B varias calles.
- ☐ C unos puestos.
- ☐ D toda la zona.

(v) El regalo que Marcos dio a su amiga…

- ☐ A tenía mucho valor.
- ☐ B costó mucho dinero.
- ☐ C era muy barato.
- ☐ D era nuevo.

(5 marks)

Review your skills

Check up

Review your responses to the exam-style questions on pages 39 and 40. Tick ⊘ the column that shows how well you think you have done each of the following.

	Not quite ⊘	Nearly there ⊘	Got it! ⊘
identified the way words relate to each other in a sentence	☐	☐	☐
made use of tenses to clarify meaning	☐	☐	☐
made use of pronouns to clarify meaning	☐	☐	☐

Need more practice?

Go back to pages 34 and 35 and complete ⊘ the two exam-style questions there. Use the checklist to help you.

Checklist In my answers, do I...	⊘
read the introduction to the question in order to understand the context and predict the vocabulary?	
read through the text *and* the questions?	
analyse the sentences, looking for verb, subject, complement or description, to help my understanding?	
identify the tenses in the sentences?	
identify pronouns (reflexive, direct or indirect object) that can help make sense of the text?	

Remember that in an exam situation you should focus on answering the questions. Don't worry about the parts of the text that are not relevant to those questions.

How confident do you feel about each of these **skills**? Colour in ⊘ the bars.

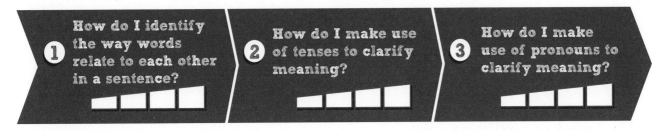

1 How do I identify the way words relate to each other in a sentence?

2 How do I make use of tenses to clarify meaning?

3 How do I make use of pronouns to clarify meaning?

⑥ Giving clear answers with appropriate detail

This unit will help you to learn how to make sure you give clear answers with just the right amount of detail required. The skills you will build are to:

- sidestep wrong, ambiguous or contradictory answers
- produce answers that are sufficiently detailed
- avoid including irrelevant information.

In the exam, you will be asked to do reading tasks similar to the one below. This unit will prepare you to tackle these questions and write the best answers in English.

Do not answer this question yet. You will be asked to come back to it at the end of the unit.

Exam-style question

Eating out

(a) Read this review of a restaurant.

> En el barrio madrileño de Chamberí, cerca de la estación de tren, se encuentra un espectacular restaurante que te recibe con trato familiar y agradable hasta en el nombre, *Flor de Amor*.
>
> Tienes que visitar este lugar si buscas un estilo completamente diferente y moderno donde puedes gozar de recetas sencillas de la cocina tradicional francesa.

Answer the following questions **in English**. You do not need to write full sentences.

(i) Where is the restaurant close to?

.... (1)

(ii) What sort of welcome will you receive?

.... (1)

(iii) What sort of food does the restaurant serve?

.... (1)

(b) The review continues.

> Ofrecemos un 40% de descuento si consumes como mínimo un primero y un segundo. Disfruta de nuestra promoción de lunes a viernes en comidas y los sábados y domingos en cenas. *Flor de Amor* es una gran elección para todas las ocasiones. Visítanos.

(i) How many courses do you need to order to get a discount?

.... (1)

(ii) What meal is on special offer on weekdays?

.... (1)

(5 marks)

In exam tasks there are different styles of questions: some require you to pick the exact information from the text, others ask you to make deductions. It is important to learn to identify the different question types as it can help you select the appropriate information from the text.

(1) Look at the three questions in the exam-style task below. Write what style of questions they are: deduction or fact? ....

Do not answer this question yet. You will be asked to come back to it at the end of the unit.

Exam-style question

Celebrations and festivals

Read the article below.

> Cumpleaños, aniversarios, fiestas de navidad… Si nos paramos a pensar por un momento en
> todas las ocasiones en las que podríamos derrochar dinero, nos entraría un ataque de nervios. Normalmente creemos que gastar mucho dinero es necesario para demostrar el aprecio hacia una persona.
>
> Sin embargo, un regalo no tiene por qué ser caro y dará el mismo placer o más que otro con un precio alto. El día de mi cumpleaños mi hermano menor se pasó una tarde entera haciéndome una tarjeta preciosa. Este detalle tan personal me encantó. ¡Me gustó más que todos los demás regalos que recibí!

Answer the following questions **in English**.

(a) What did the writer's brother do for her birthday?

.... (1)

(b) What did the writer think of her brother's gesture?

.... (1)

(c) Summarise the writer's feeling about giving presents.

.... (1)

(3 marks)

The three key questions in the **skills boosts** will help you improve how you answer these types of questions.

 1 How do I sidestep wrong, ambiguous or contradictory answers?

 2 How do I produce answers that are sufficiently detailed?

 3 How do I avoid including irrelevant information?

How do I sidestep wrong, ambiguous and contradictory answers?

You need to make sure the answers you give make sense. First make sure you know what the questions are asking. Then select the exact bit of information in the text, make sure you understand it and choose the correct option.

① Read the following descriptions and the questions that follow each one. Tick ✓ the correct answer and note 🖉 on paper why the others are wrong.

Example:

> Anoche cenamos en un restaurante italiano que está muy cerca de mi casa. Prefiero la comida china, pero fuimos para celebrar el cumpleaños de mi abuela. Nos gustaron mucho los postres. **Carmela**

Why did Carmela go to the restaurant with her family?

i ☐ She likes Italian (*italiano*) food. *Contradicts the text; she prefers Chinese food.*

ii ☐ It's close (*cerca*) to home. *Ambiguous; the restaurant just happens to be close to her home.*

iii ✓ It was her grandmother's birthday (*cumpleaños*).

iv ☐ She likes to eat desserts (*postres*). *The question asks 'why' and this is not the reason. The family enjoyed the desserts, but that's a result.*

Be careful: just because a word appears in the text as well as in the question, that doesn't mean it's the answer. To help you pick out the correct answer, look at the question word.

If a question begins with:

- 'why' – look for vocabulary that suggests a reason (*porque, para*).
- 'when' – look for times and dates.   • 'what' – look for verbs and nouns.
- 'where' – look for locations and places.   • 'who' – look for vocabulary related to people.

a

> Normalmente mis padres y yo celebramos la Nochevieja en casa, aunque a veces voy a una fiesta con amigos. Sin embargo, este año vamos a Colombia, donde se reunirá toda la familia para una gran cena. **Xiomara**

How is Xiomara planning to spend New Year's Eve?

i ☐ She is staying at home with her parents.   iii ☐ She is going to a party.

ii ☐ She is celebrating with a dinner with friends.   iv ☐ She's planning to be in Colombia.

b

> Me gusta preparar la comida. Cocino de todo: pescado, sopas, pasteles. Lo que más me gusta hacer es tortilla de patatas, aunque no me gustan mucho los huevos. **Carlitos**

What does Carlitos like to cook the most?

i ☐ lunch   iii ☐ tortilla

ii ☐ fish, soup and cakes   iv ☐ eggs

How do I produce answers that are sufficiently detailed?

Your answers must give the exact information needed to answer the questions, so you must ensure that you have included all relevant details from the text.

① Read the question after each section of the text about Sofía's visit to a festival in Valencia. Check you understand the wrong answer that is given and the examiner's comment. Then write ✎ the correct answer.

> Este marzo fui a Valencia para ver la famosa fiesta de Las Fallas. Quería estar los <u>veinte días</u> que dura la fiesta, pero sólo me quedé <u>una semana</u> porque tenía que trabajar.

The question is asking 'how long' Sofia wanted to stay so look for words to do with time in the text.

Example: <u>How long</u> did Sofía want to stay in Valencia?

~~20~~ insufficient detail: 20 hours, days, weeks or months?

<u>20 days</u>

Always look at the question words to help you give a complete answer. Here the question is about duration.

> Me encantaron los concursos de paella. Probé muchos platos y algunos estaban riquísimos; otros no tanto <u>porque es difícil hacer una paella en la calle para tanta gente</u>.

a <u>Why</u> weren't all the paella dishes tasty? Give **two** details.

Difficult to make a paella. insufficient detail

....

The question word (Why) is asking for reasons, so look for vocabulary that suggests a reason and the actual reason(s) given in the text.

> Durante el día había desfiles y danzas tradicionales muy bonitos. Por la noche hacían castillos de fuegos artificiales en la plaza que para mí eran aún más espectaculares.

b Why did she prefer the evening activities?

During the day they had parades and dances that were nice. At night they made firework castles in the square which were even more spectacular. Too much detail; answer is buried.

....

> Todas las noches también había música y el sábado bailamos hasta la madrugada. Sin embargo, lo mejor para mí fue la última noche cuando quemaron figuras enormes de escenas cómicas y de personas famosas.

c Which was the best evening in Sofía's opinion?

last night Last night or <u>the</u> last night? Insufficient detail, therefore ambiguous.

....

③ How do I avoid including irrelevant information?

When answering a question, you must avoid writing too little and not giving enough detail, but equally you must avoid writing too much and risk being penalised for an ambiguous or unclear answer. Also, make sure you are not answering a different question from the one set!

① Read this article about a film festival and find the five sections of the text with the relevant information to answer each question. Write 🖉 the letter of the question in the box after that section.

> La Fiesta del Cine se celebra a partir de este lunes 8 de mayo hasta el miércoles día 10 ☐ en salas de toda España ☐ *a* ☐, con entradas a solo 2,90 euros ☐. Para conseguir precios reducidos se debe registrar en la página web www.fiestadelcine.com ☐. Las entradas están ya a la venta ☐ en las taquillas de los cines participantes y por Internet ☐. Se estima que 2,6 millones de personas asistirán al festival ☐, medio millón más que el año pasado ☐, a pesar de que competirá con la celebración de los partidos de semifinales de la Liga de Campeones de fútbol los últimos dos días ☐.

- **a** Where is the festival taking place?
- **b** What can you get if you register online?
- **c** Give **two** places where you can buy tickets.
- **d** How many more people will go this year compared to last year?
- **e** What else is happening at the same time as the festival?

② Read Andrés' message about a festival. Look at the answers to the questions and cross out (ᴄᴀᴛ) the information that is not relevant. Write 🖉 why it is not relevant.

> Remember that for this sort of task, the information will come in the order of the questions.

> En agosto voy al Festival Internacional de Deportes Extremos en Galicia. Dura tres días y es la competición más grande de deportes extremos en España. Vienen participantes de todas partes del mundo a demostrar sus habilidades. También hay talleres donde puedes aprender algunas de las técnicas deportivas de la mano de los profesionales. Voy porque el festival no solo es deportivo, sino también cultural. Ofrece una gran variedad de espectáculos artísticos, bandas en vivo y DJs.

Example:

| What type of festival is Andrés going to? |

He's going to an extreme sports festival ~~in Galicia~~.

The question doesn't ask about where the festival takes place.

> Don't forget to use the question word to identify the relevant detail. Here the question is asking what type of festival the person is going to, so where the festival is taking place is irrelevant.

a | How big is the festival? |

It's the biggest in Spain ~~and lasts 3 days~~. ....

b | Where do the contestants come from? |

They come from all over the world to demonstrate their skills. ....

c | What can you learn in the workshops? |

sports skills at the hands of the experts ....

③ Now go back to ① and write 🖉 your answers to questions a–e on paper.

Your turn!

Here is an exam-style question which requires you to put into practice the skills you have worked on, specifically how to make your answers as clear and appropriately detailed as possible. Too little or too much information could cost you marks! ✏

Christmas Eve

(a) Read this blog by Danuta about Christmas Eve in Spain and Poland.

> Soy polaca, pero vivo en España y en los dos países el día más importante de Navidad es el 24 de diciembre cuando se reúne toda la familia. En Polonia lo primero que hacemos es buscar la primera estrella en el cielo y después ya la fiesta empieza en serio. Compartimos un pan especial y lo bonito es que damos el pan sagrado a los animales de la casa ya que, según la tradición, en esa noche los animales hablan el lenguaje humano. Esto no se hace en España.

Answer the following questions **in English**. You do not need to write in full sentences.

(i) Who gets together on Christmas Eve in Spain and Poland?

.... **(1)**

(ii) What don't Spanish families look for on Christmas Eve?

.... **(1)**

(iii) What do Polish people believe animals can do on Christmas Eve?

.... **(1)**

(b) The blog continues.

> Luego la familia se sienta a la mesa a compartir la cena navideña igual que nuestros vecinos españoles. Sin embargo, los polacos dejamos una silla libre y un plato vacío por si alguien llama a la puerta.
>
> A medianoche vamos a la iglesia como se hace en España. Lo que echo de menos es que en Polonia, después de la misa, hay grupos de jóvenes, disfrazados de animales, que van de casa en casa para cantar villancicos y a cambio de eso hay que darles dulces o dinero.

(i) What do both Polish and Spanish families do at midnight on Christmas Eve?

.... **(1)**

(ii) Name **one** thing carol singers are given in Poland.

.... **(1)**

(5 marks)

Don't forget to look at the question words 'who', 'what', 'why', 'when' and 'where' in the question to help you locate your answer in the text.

Your turn!

Here is an exam-style question which requires you to put into practice the skills you have worked on, specifically how to ensure that your answers are sufficiently detailed without including irrelevant information. ✏

Exam-style question

Eating cheaply

Read Diego's blog post below.

> ✏   — □ ✕
>
> Si quieres ahorrar dinero que gastas en alimentación, es posible comer bien en casa por menos de 2 euros al día. Creo que tiramos mucho dinero y muchísima comida. Nos obsesionan las marcas y tenemos miedo de los productos baratos. En mi pueblo es más fácil encontrar un mango de la India que fruta fresca de la zona. Pero, sobre todo, creo que estamos obsesionados por la proteína animal. Comer tanta carne no es sostenible en términos ambientales y desde luego tampoco en términos de salud. Y desde el punto de vista económico, es un sobrecoste innecesario. ¿No será mejor reducir el consumo de carne y remplazarlo de vez en cuando con legumbres?

Answer the following questions **in English**.

(a) Where does Diego find it hard to find locally grown fruit?

.... (1)

(b) What does he say is unsustainable?

.... (1)

(c) Summarise how Diego thinks we can eat more cheaply.

.... (1)

(3 marks)

> Remember that even if a word in the question appears in the text, that does not mean it is definitely the answer. Read the text closely so you do not miss a negation, for instance, which changes the meaning of a sentence.

> Some questions may require you to deduce the information. For instance, the answer for question (c) is not spelled out in the text.

Review your skills

Check up

Review your responses to the exam-style questions on pages 47 and 48. Tick ✓ the column that shows how well you think you have done each of the following.

	Not quite ✓	Nearly there ✓	Got it! ✓
sidestepped wrong, ambiguous and contradictory answers	☐	☐	☐
produced answers that are sufficiently detailed	☐	☐	☐
avoided including irrelevant information	☐	☐	☐

Need more practice?

Go back to pages 42 and 43 and complete ✐ the two exam-style questions there. Use the checklist to help you.

Checklist In my answers, do I...	✓
make sure I have located the answer in the relevant part of the text?	
ensure I haven't used words that are in the text but don't address the question?	
give enough details to make sure the question is answered fully?	
avoid giving too much information in case it is irrelevant?	

Remember to read the instructions carefully. When giving your answer, do not write full sentences if you don't need to, as it won't increase your mark. On the contrary, you might lose marks if you're not careful, as you run the risk of making your answer unclear or ambiguous. Once you're confident you know the answer, write it in as few words as possible.

How confident do you feel about each of these **skills**? Colour in ✐ the bars.

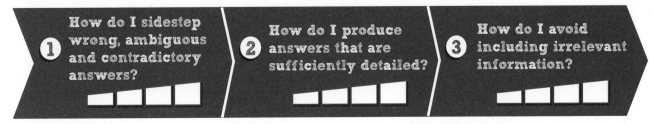

1. How do I sidestep wrong, ambiguous and contradictory answers?

2. How do I produce answers that are sufficiently detailed?

3. How do I avoid including irrelevant information?

⑦ Inferring meaning

This unit will help you to learn how to understand implied meaning and opinions. The skills you will build are to:

- infer implied meaning
- use inference to identify opinions and justifications
- make connections between different parts of a text to understand meaning.

In the exam, you will be asked to do reading tasks similar to the ones below. This unit will prepare you to tackle these questions and use inference to come up with the correct answers.

'Inference' means a conclusion you come to, based on the information you have. You use inference to understand meaning that is implied when an idea or opinion is suggested but not stated directly.

Do not answer this question yet. You will be asked to come back to it at the end of the unit.

Exam-style question

Ofertas de empleo

Lee esta información sobre puestos vacantes.

> **Un hotel en Ibiza**
> Buscamos personal de cocina para trabajar en el restaurante. Debes tener buen nivel de dos (o más) idiomas. Experiencia en el mundo de la restauración será una ventaja.
>
> **Grandes almacenes deportivos**
> Tienda de ropa y equipo deportivo busca jóvenes para trabajar de mediados de julio a finales de agosto. Necesitas buena presencia y aptitudes de comunicación para relacionarte con los clientes.
>
> **Campamento de verano**
> Se buscan monitores para este verano para trabajar en un entorno natural. No necesitas experiencia, pero debes tener una personalidad abierta y positiva. Vivirás en el campamento y animarás a los niños a participar en actividades deportivas y creativas.
>
> **Empresa de marketing**
> Buscamos a dos jóvenes para realizar tareas administrativas durante el verano. No hace falta tener experiencia de trabajo en una oficina, pero se requieren conocimientos de Word, Photoshop y Excel.

¿Cuál es el mejor trabajo para cada persona? Escoge entre **Un hotel en Ibiza**, **Grandes almacenes deportivos**, **Campamento de verano** o **Empresa de marketing**. Puedes usar los trabajos más de una vez.

Ejemplo: Me gustaría trabajar de dependienta.   *Grandes almacenes*

(a) No me van bien los idiomas, pero me encanta la informática. .... (1)

(b) Soy activa y deportista. En el futuro voy a ser o profesora o maestra. .... (1)

(c) Quiero trabajar en turismo. Domino el inglés y el francés. .... (1)

(d) Prefiero el campo a la ciudad. Quiero trabajar al aire libre. .... (1)

(e) Me interesa la comida y me encanta cocinar. .... (1)

(5 marks)

Do not answer this question yet. You will be asked to come back to it at the end of the unit.

Exam-style question

Los jóvenes españoles encuentran empleo en el extranjero

Lee este artículo.

El porcentaje de menores de 25 años desempleados es alrededor del 42%. No es de sorprender entonces que el año pasado, casi 100,000 jóvenes buscaron empleo fuera de España, en Europa, Estados Unidos y Australia.

Oriana Torres, 19 años y de Sevilla, nos contó que encontró un puesto de trabajo en una cafetería en Londres. "Trabajo muchas horas y las tareas son repetitivas: preparo y sirvo café y té desde las 7 de la mañana hasta las 5 de la tarde. Lo bueno es que me llevo bien con mis compañeros de trabajo: son todos muy simpáticos. A veces hay clientes impacientes, que es un poco estresante, pero por lo general, la gente es muy amable. Una ventaja de trabajar aquí es que tengo que hablar inglés todo el día. Al principio no entendía nada, pero ahora hablo bastante bien."

Pon una cruz [X] en la casilla correcta.

Ejemplo: Muchos jóvenes españoles van a otros países…

- [ ] A de vacaciones.
- [ ] B a estudiar.
- [x] C a trabajar.
- [ ] D a aprender inglés.

(i) Oriana Torres trabaja ahora en…

- [ ] A España.
- [ ] B Inglaterra.
- [ ] C Estados Unidos.
- [ ] D Australia.

(ii) Oriana Torres trabaja de…

- [ ] A enfermera.
- [ ] B recepcionista.
- [ ] C cocinera.
- [ ] D camarera.

(iii) El aspecto negativo del trabajo es que…

- [ ] A gana poco dinero.
- [ ] B no le gustan sus colegas.
- [ ] C hace lo mismo todos los días.
- [ ] D su jefe es severo.

(iv) La mayoría de los clientes son…

- [ ] A agradables.
- [ ] B mal educados.
- [ ] C impacientes.
- [ ] D antipáticos.

(v) Lo bueno del trabajo es que…

- [ ] A conoce a mucha gente.
- [ ] B le gusta el café.
- [ ] C no se aburre.
- [ ] D ha mejorado su nivel de inglés.

The three key questions in the **skills boosts** will help you improve how you answer these types of questions.

1 How do I infer implied meaning?

2 How do I use inference to identify opinions and justifications?

3 How do I make connections between different parts of a text to understand meaning?

1 How do I infer implied meaning?

For some exam tasks, you will need to show that you can identify and understand positive and negative ideas. To prepare for this, learn key words and phrases from each topic. Also, focus on words and phrases that express positive or negative ideas.

1 Read the adjectives you might use to describe work. Are they positive or negative? Write 🖉 'P' for positive or 'N' for negative beside each one.

- **a** variado ☐
- **b** duro ☐
- **c** fácil ☐
- **d** interesante ☐

- **e** repetitivo ☐
- **f** útil ☐
- **g** difícil ☐
- **h** creativo ☐

- **i** aburrido ☐
- **j** divertido ☐
- **k** emocionante ☐
- **l** monótono ☐

2 Match the Spanish verbs to the English verbs. Then tick ✓ the Spanish verbs that you might use to express a positive idea about work and put a cross ✗ beside any that express a negative idea.

☐ A aprender	a to be bored
☐ B aburrirse	b to earn (money)
☐ C ayudar	c to help
☐ D ganar (dinero)	d to improve
☐ E mejorar	e to learn
☐ F viajar	f to travel

3 Read the sentences. Underline Ⓐ the positive ideas and circle Ⓐ the negative ideas. 🖉

- **a** <u>El sueldo es muy alto</u>, pero tienes que (trabajar muchas horas).
- **b** El horario es flexible y lo bueno es que tienes los fines de semana libres.
- **c** El jefe es bastante severo, pero nos explica bien las tareas.
- **d** El trabajo no era difícil, pero llegó a ser monótono.
- **e** Lo mejor de las prácticas fue que aprendí mucho. Fue una experiencia útil.
- **f** Gané muy poco dinero, pero mejoré mi nivel de español.
- **g** El trabajo no era interesante. Fue una pérdida de tiempo.

> Look out for words and phrases that introduce a positive or negative idea.
>
> **Positive:** lo bueno, lo mejor, la ventaja, afortunadamente, ¡menos mal!
>
> **Negative:** lo malo, lo peor, la desventaja, desafortunadamente

② How do I use inference to identify opinions and justifications?

The texts you have to read often combine opinions with justifications, i.e. reasons or examples. If you are not sure you have understood the writer's opinion, look for reasons or examples that can give you clues.

> To identify opinions in a text, look out for verbs that are connected with ideas (*pensar, creer, decir*).

① Underline Ⓐ the word or phrase in each sentence which introduces an opinion.

a Creo que es importante aprender idiomas. **Noemí**

b Nuestros profesores piensan que vale la pena hacer prácticas laborales. **David**

c En mi opinión, no es necesario pasar la aspiradora todos los días. **Julia**

d Mi abuelo dice que no importa qué haces, sino cómo lo haces. **Raúl**

e Para mí, lo más importante es hacer un trabajo útil. **Luisa**

> Also, look for words and phrases that imply opinions and learn them in pairs of antonyms. For example: *¡qué bien!* (that's great!) – *¡qué pena!* (what a pity!); *estoy de acuerdo* (I agree) – *no estoy de acuerdo* (I disagree).

② Underline Ⓐ the correct option to match the sense of the rest of the sentence.

a Si quieres trabajar en el extranjero, es *una ventaja / una desventaja* no hablar otros idiomas.

b Hacer prácticas laborales *vale la pena / es una pérdida de tiempo* porque puedes aprender mucho.

c Me gustaría ser médico o veterinario, pero *afortunadamente / desafortunadamente* no saco buenas notas en ciencias.

d Hacer un curso de primeros auxilios es *una buena idea / una mala idea* para los que hacen de canguro.

e *Admiro / No aguanto* a los que trabajan de bomberos o policías porque son valientes y ayudan a la gente.

③ Read what Miguel says about his job. Which of the following ideas are implied in the text? Put a tick ✓ for 'implied in the text' and a cross ✗ for 'not implied in the text'.

> *Creo que tengo mucha suerte porque tengo un trabajo que me encanta. Me chifla el deporte y soy profesor de educación física. Lo que más me gusta es ver cómo los chicos se divierten cuando hacen deporte y cómo aprenden a trabajar en equipo y llevarse bien con sus compañeros. Además, pienso que la actividad física ayuda a los jóvenes a estudiar mejor y a tener más confianza en sí mismos. El aspecto negativo es que siempre hay algunos estudiantes que no quieren trabajar, pero afortunadamente, son una minoría.*

Example: Miguel works as a teacher. ✓

a He loves his work.

b He thinks playing sport helps students to learn how to follow rules.

c He gets job satisfaction from seeing positive results.

d He thinks that sport is beneficial for young people.

e He doesn't like teaching students who don't like sport.

f He finds that only a small number of students have a negative attitude.

3 **How do I make connections between different parts of a text to understand meaning?**

You need to read and understand all of the text in an exam task to make sure you can answer the questions correctly. Always read texts and questions carefully to find the clues and connections to help you answer accurately.

1 **a** Read the Spanish statements and annotate ✐ the key language in English.

loves IT

i No me van los idiomas, pero me encanta la informática. ....

ii Me gustaría trabajar de dependienta. ....

iii Soy activa y deportista. En el futuro voy a ser o profesora o maestra. ....

iv Quiero trabajar en turismo. Domino el inglés y el francés. ....

v Me interesa la comida y me encanta cocinar. ....

vi Prefiero el campo a la ciudad. Quiero trabajar al aire libre. ....

b Highlight ✐ all the language in the four job advertisements below that relates to each sentence from **a**. Write down ✐ the number of the relevant sentence next to each piece of highlighted text.

A Un hotel en Ibiza
Buscamos personal de cocina para trabajar en el restaurante. Debes tener
i buen nivel de dos o más idiomas. Experiencia en el mundo de la restauración será una ventaja.

B Grandes almacenes deportivos
Tienda de ropa y equipo deportivo busca jóvenes para trabajar de mediados de julio a finales de agosto. Necesitas buena presencia y aptitudes de comunicación con los clientes.

C Campamento de verano
Se buscan monitores para trabajar en un entorno natural para este verano. No necesitas experiencia, pero debes tener una personalidad abierta y positiva. Vivirás en el campamento y animarás a los niños a participar en actividades deportivas y creativas.

D Empresa de marketing
Buscamos a dos jóvenes para realizar tareas administrativas durante el verano. No hace falta tener experiencia de trabajo en una oficina, pero se requieren conocimientos de Word, *i* Photoshop y Excel.

c Using all the information you've gathered from looking at all the texts, write ✐ the letter of the appropriate advertisement (A–D) next to each sentence in **a**.

Your turn!

Here is an exam-style question for you to practise the skills you have worked on, specifically how to show that you can use ideas and information to make connections between different parts of a text.

A gap year

Read the article below.

> Tomarse un año sabático empieza a ser una práctica más común en España. Al terminar los estudios en el instituto, muchos jóvenes no saben qué estudiar en la universidad y pasar un año fuera del sistema educativo les ofrece enriquecedoras oportunidades.
>
> Isabel Hernández, 18 años y de Madrid, nos dijo que fue a estudiar inglés a Australia durante un año. Ahora ha vuelto e irá a la universidad a estudiar arquitectura. Dice que la experiencia le ayudó a mejorar su nivel de inglés y a ser más independiente y más responsable.
>
> "Tomarse un año para trabajar y viajar trae ventajas," dice María Luisa Bertrán, profesora de psicología. "Viajar, conocer otras culturas y aprender idiomas ayuda a los jóvenes. Aprenden a comunicarse y a adaptarse mejor, a trabajar en equipo y a tener una perspectiva más abierta del mundo."

Answer the following questions **in English**.

(a) Is taking a gap year a long-established tradition in Spain or is it relatively new?

.... (1)

(b) What did Isabel Hernández gain from her gap year?

.... (1)

(c) Summarise why Spanish students are choosing to take a gap year and the benefits.

.... (1)

(3 marks)

Notice that the answer to question (a) is not given directly in the text. Look at the first sentence of the text and work out what it implies about gap years in Spain.

To be able to answer question (c), you need to find information in all three paragraphs.

Your turn!

Here is an exam-style question for you to practise the skills you have worked on, specifically how to use inference to identify opinions and justifications. ✐

Exam-style question

Summer holiday jobs

(a) Read this extract from a web page about holiday jobs.

> Puedes encontrar trabajo de dependientes/as en las tiendas de ropa y en los grandes almacenes. Se necesita gente para trabajar durante el verano y sustituir a los empleados que se van de vacaciones. Debes tener buena presencia y la habilidad de comunicarte con los clientes. Saber hablar inglés, francés o alemán sería una ventaja. Lo bueno: recibirás descuentos (podrás comprar, por ejemplo, ropa a precios reducidos).
> Lo malo: tendrás que trabajar los fines de semana.

Answer the following questions **in English**. You do not need to write in full sentences.

(i)   What would you be doing if you applied for these jobs?

.... **(1)**

(ii) Why are extra staff needed at this time of year?

.... **(1)**

(iii) Give one advantage or disadvantage of the job.

.... **(1)**

(b) The web page continues.

> En Cinemundo, hay trabajo para jóvenes y estudiantes. Debes tener 16 años o más. Trabajarás sólo 4 horas al día y cambiarás de tarea cada día. Un día venderás entradas, al día siguiente venderás refrescos y dulces, y así sucesivamente. Así que el trabajo es variado y puedes ver las películas gratis, pero el sueldo es bajo.

(i)   Who can apply for this work?

.... **(1)**

(ii) Give one advantage or disadvantage of the job.

.... **(1)**

(5 marks)

Notice that you will need to infer what is implied in the text to answer the first question. The text tells you the job title and the place, so from that you have to infer what the work would be.

Look for words and phrases that introduce positive and negative ideas. These will help you to find the answers about the advantages and disadvantages of the jobs.

Review your skills

Check up

Review your responses to the exam-style questions on pages 55 and 56. Tick ✓ the column that shows how well you think you have done each of the following.

	Not quite ✓	Nearly there ✓	Got it! ✓
inferred implied meaning	☐	☐	☐
used inference to identify opinions and justifications	☐	☐	☐
made connections between different parts of a text to understand meaning	☐	☐	☐

Need more practice?

Go back to pages 50 and 51 and complete ✐ the two exam-style questions there. Use the checklist to help you.

> In reading tasks, you will often find that the questions and the text use different words and phrases to refer to the same ideas and information. Knowing the vocabulary for each topic will help you to identify the connections between the text and the questions and understand the implied meaning.

Checklist In my answers, do I...	✓
identify words and phrases that express ideas, thoughts and opinions?	
recognise words and phrases that introduce a positive or negative opinion?	
identify and understand positive and negative opinions?	
identify words and phrases that imply opinions?	
use inference to understand implied meaning?	
connect information from different parts of the texts to infer meaning?	

How confident do you feel about each of these **skills**? Colour in ✐ the bars.

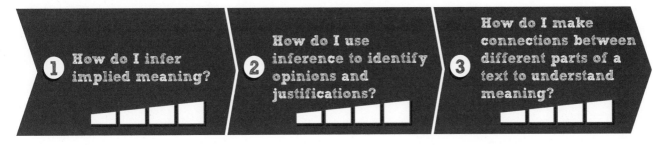

1. How do I infer implied meaning?

2. How do I use inference to identify opinions and justifications?

3. How do I make connections between different parts of a text to understand meaning?

Translating accurately into English

This unit will help you to improve your accuracy when translating from Spanish into English. The skills you will build are to:

- make sure you include all key details
- avoid including superfluous material
- avoid distorting the meaning of sentences.

In the exam, you will be asked to do a translation task similar to the ones below. This unit will prepare you to tackle translating carefully and accurately.

> The key to getting good marks for translating a passage like this is to look carefully at the detail and to make sure you include it all in your translation. Look at the verbs to get the tense right (present, past, future). Look at the adjectives: *un pueblo pequeño, el viaje largo*. Make sure you include all the information. In this passage, for example, include all the family members mentioned: *mis padres, mi hermana, mis tíos, mis primos*.

Do not answer this question yet. You will be asked to come back to it at the end of the unit.

Exam-style question

Translation

Translate this passage **into English**.

> Vivo en un pueblo pequeño en el norte de España. Me gusta nadar y me gusta la gimnasia.
> El año pasado fui de vacaciones a Francia con mis padres, mi hermana, mis tíos y mis primos.
> Fuimos en coche y el viaje fue bastante largo, pero lo pasamos muy bien. Este año, iré a un
> campamento de verano en las montañas con mi hermana.

....

....

....

....

....

(7 marks)

1. Look at a student's attempt at this exam-style translation. He has made several mistakes. Look through the comments. Underline Ⓐ the problems in his text.

Do not answer this question yet. You will be asked to come back to it at the end of the unit.

Translation

Translate this passage **into English**.

En febrero, organizamos una carrera solidaria de bici en mi pueblo. Participaron más de cincuenta personas. Hacía bastante frío y hacía viento pero, a pesar del mal tiempo, lo pasamos bien. Después desayunamos todos en el bar del pueblo. Vamos a repetir la carrera el año que viene.

....

....

....

....

(7 marks)

- Verb tense is incorrect (–ar verbs have the same form for 'we' plural in the present and the preterite, so you need to look at other verbs to see if they're in the past or present, e.g. *participaron*).

- A word (*charity*) is missing, so not all the information is given.

- An unknown expression, which could have been understood in context, was left out.

In February, we are organising a bike race in my village.

a They took part more of 50 people.

b It was quite cold and it was windy, but we had a good time.

c Afterwards, we all had breakfast in the bar of the village.

d We are going to do the race again the year coming.

- The word order in the sentence is not correct in English.

- An expression is translated word for word and does not make sense in English.

- An expression is translated word for word and does not sound natural in English.

- An expression is translated word for word and does not sound natural in English.

The three key questions in the **skills boosts** will help you improve how you answer these types of questions.

1 How do I make sure I include all key details?

2 How do I avoid including superfluous material?

3 How do I avoid distorting the meaning of sentences?

> **1** How do I make sure I include all key details?

To make sure you include all the key elements, you must check that every piece of information in the Spanish text appears in your translation.

- Look for **time expressions** in texts and make sure you include them in your translation.
- Also, make sure you include the phrases that tell you **how often** something happens: *a veces, siempre,* etc.
- Remember to translate '**intensifiers**' (words such as *muy, demasiado,* etc.).

(1) Highlight the word or expression in each Spanish sentence that is missed out in the English translation. Then add the missing words or expressions to the English translation.

Example: El ciclismo es muy popular ahora.   Cycling is very popular ⌃.   [now]

a Fuimos de excursión a las montañas hace dos semanas.

We went on a trip to the mountains.

b En las grandes ciudades hay demasiada gente sin hogar.

In the big cities there are homeless people.

c Beber demasiado alcohol es un problema bastante serio.

Drinking alcohol is quite a serious problem.

d Tomar drogas es mucho más peligroso.

Taking drugs is more dangerous.

(2) Read the Spanish text in the exam-style question and a student's English translation. Compare the translation with the text. There are five details missing.

Translate this passage **into English**.

Me encanta el deporte y normalmente practico algún deporte todos los días. Casi nunca veo la tele porque es aburrido, pero hace poco vi un campeonato de atletismo en que una atleta de mi región ganó una medalla. Fue muy emocionante. El año que viene me gustaría participar en un triatlón.

(7 marks)

[usually]

I love sport and I ⌃ do some kind of sport every day. I never watch TV because it's boring, but I watched an athletics championship in which an athlete from my area won a medal. It was exciting. I would like to take part in a triatlón.

a Highlight the five words or phrases in the Spanish text that are not included in the English translation. The first one has been done for you.

b Show where the details should appear in the English translation and write them in.

② How do I avoid including superfluous material?

If you try to translate word for word, you will end up adding words or phrases in your translation that aren't necessary in English. Instead you need to think of the English equivalent of Spanish expressions.

① Read the Spanish sentences and highlight 🖊 the words that are unnecessary in the English translations.

a Creo que el problema más preocupante es el calentamiento global.

I think that the most worrying problem is `the` *climate change.*

b Debemos animar a todos a reciclar más.

We should encourage to everyone to recycle more.

c Voy al instituto en bici o a pie todos los días.

I go to the school by bike or on foot every day.

d Acabamos de leer un reportaje interesante sobre energía renovable.

We have just of read an interesting report about renewable energy.

e No se debe tirar la basura al suelo.

You shouldn't throw litter onto the ground.

f La contaminación del aire es un problema grave en las grandes ciudades.

The pollution of the air in big cities is a serious problem.

g Hay que proteger los animales amenazados.

We should protect animals in danger of extinction.

② Read the sentences in Spanish and write 🖊 a word or words in the gaps to complete the English translations.

a Vivo en una ciudad industrial al norte de Barcelona.

I live in an industrial city .... Barcelona.

b El problema del medio ambiente que más me preocupa es la contaminación del aire.

The environmental problem that worries me most is ....

c Hay demasiados coches y camiones en el centro de la ciudad.

There are too many cars and trucks in ....

d Debemos usar el transporte público o ir a pie.

We should use .... or go on foot.

e Hay que informar al público de la importancia de cuidar el medio ambiente.

We must inform .... the importance of looking after the environment.

3 **How do I avoid distorting the meaning of sentences?**

Wrongly translating a word or phrase can change the meaning of a sentence, so you need to be as accurate as possible. Focus on the words and phrases you know and keep guesswork to a minimum.

1 **a** Read the Spanish text. A student has translated it, but has left gaps because she didn't know some of the words. Highlight ✏ the words in the Spanish text that haven't been translated.

> En casa hacemos todo lo posible para ahorrar energía. En invierno, solamente usamos la calefacción cuando hace mucho frío. En verano, cerramos las cortinas y las persianas durante el día y la casa se queda fresca por dentro. De esta manera, usamos los ventiladores únicamente cuando hace mucho calor. Además, tenemos placas solares en el tejado para calentar el agua.

At home we do everything we can to save energy. In winter, we use the

i .... *only when it's very cold. In summer, we*

close the curtains and the **ii** .... *during the*

day and the house stays cool inside. This way, we use the

iii .... *only when it's very hot. In addition, we*

have **iv** .... *on the* **v** .... *to heat the water.*

> If there is a word or phrase you don't know, don't make a wild guess. Look at the context and use your powers of logic and deduction to work out the meaning.

b Read the English translation in **a** again and write ✏ the correct word from the options below in each gap. Look at the context each time to see which word makes most sense. Note down ✏ what helped you to decide.

i cooker	gas fire	heating	*We use it only when it's very cold.*
ii windows	blinds	carpets	....
iii fans	radiators	freezer	....
iv sunshades	solar panels	double glazing	....
v garden	terrace	roof	....

2 Highlight ✏ the words or phrases that are incorrectly translated in these sentences. (**Clue:** they don't make sense!) Then correct ✏ them, as in the example.

Example: Tener una dieta sana y hacer deporte es importante para la salud.

Going on a ~~crazy~~ diet and doing sport is important for good health. <u>healthy</u> ....

a Voy a comer más ensalada, verduras y fruta.

I'm going to eat more salad, leaves and fruit. ....

b Me gustan las manzanas, pero no me gustan las peras.

I like apples, but I don't like hot dogs. ....

c Vivimos en un barrio en las afueras de la ciudad y hay mucho tráfico.

We live in a bar in the outskirts of the city and there is a lot of traffic. ....

d Hay que apagar las luces para ahorrar energía.

We must switch on the lights to save energy. ....

Your turn!

Here is an exam-style question for you to practise the skills you have worked on, particularly how to include all the key details. ✏️

- Read through the Spanish text before you translate it to get a general idea of what it's about.
- Then look at each sentence.
- Break each sentence down into phrases and work out what they mean and how you express them in English.

Exam-style question

Translation

Translate this passage **into English**.

> Pienso que los atletas paralímpicos son buenos modelos a seguir para los niños y los jóvenes porque luchan para superar muchas dificultades. Además, creo que vale la pena participar en eventos solidarios. Hace poco, trabajé como voluntario en una carrera ciclista en mi región que recaudó fondos para los sin techo. Fue una experiencia muy positiva.

....

....

....

....

....

(7 marks)

Notice that in Spanish, the words for 'the' (*el, la, los, las*) are used more than in English. When translating a passage like this one, think of how we would express the same phrases in English. Take the first sentence in the passage, for example. The words for 'the' are not needed in English in the first sentence (*los atletas, los niños, los jóvenes*).

Learning whole phrases that put vocabulary into context will help you with translating from Spanish. Look at the passage here and identify all the phrases you know and can translate easily before you start to write your translation.

Your turn!

Here is an exam-style question for you to practise the skills you have worked on, particularly how to avoid including superfluous material and how to avoid distorting the meaning of sentences. 🖊

Exam-style question

Translation

Translate this passage **into English**.

> Hace dos meses cambié de trabajo y ahora no tengo tiempo para ir al gimnasio ni a la piscina. Para relajarme, empecé a fumar, pero ahora necesito cambiar mi rutina para llevar una vida sana. Creo que, de lunes a viernes, voy a levantarme más temprano para correr antes de ir a la oficina. Voy a cambiar mi dieta y comer más ensalada, verduras y fruta. Además, voy a dejar de fumar.

....

....

....

....

....

(7 marks)

Be careful when translating *cambié de trabajo* and *dejar de fumar*. To avoid writing English that sounds unnatural, remember to ask yourself 'how would you say this in English?'

Be careful when you translate phrases with false friends, such as *una vida sana*, because *sana* means 'healthy', not 'sane'.

Review your skills

Check up

Review your responses to the exam-style questions on pages 63 and 64. Tick ✓ the column that shows how well you think you have done each of the following.

	Not quite ✓	Nearly there ✓	Got it! ✓
made sure I included all key details	☐	☐	☐
avoided including superfluous material	☐	☐	☐
avoided distorting the meaning of sentences	☐	☐	☐

Need more practice?

Go back to pages 58 and 59 and complete ✐ the two exam-style questions there. Use the checklist to help you.

Checklist In my answers, do I...	✓
include all the information that's in the Spanish text?	
identify and translate the verb tenses correctly?	
identify and translate the time expressions?	
identify and translate the intensifiers (muy, mucho, etc.)?	
avoid putting words and information that don't appear in the Spanish text or that aren't necessary in English?	
keep guesswork to a minimum to avoid distorting the meaning of the text?	
consider how Spanish words and phrases are expressed in English to avoid translating word for word?	

How confident do you feel about each of these **skills**? Colour in ✐ the bars.

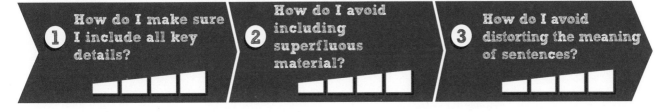

1 How do I make sure I include all key details?

2 How do I avoid including superfluous material?

3 How do I avoid distorting the meaning of sentences?

9 Using different clues to understand unfamiliar language

This unit will help you to deal with unfamiliar words and phrases. The skills you will build are to:

- use clues from the rubrics, headings and text
- use clues from the text surrounding unfamiliar words
- recognise parts of unfamiliar words.

The level of the language and tasks in this unit is a little higher than in the other units, so it will prepare you to tackle Higher level questions.

Do not answer this question yet. You will be asked to come back to it at the end of the unit.

Exam-style question

An interview with my grandmother

Read what the writer's grandmother said about changes in her lifetime.

> Mi abuela se llama Carmen. Nació en los años cuarenta, una época muy distinta a la nuestra. En aquel entonces, muchos jóvenes solían dejar la escuela a los 14 años para empezar a trabajar. Mi abuela trabajaba limpiando casas desde los 14 años hasta que se casó a los 20 años. Luego se ocupó de la casa y de los niños. Dice que su generación tenía menos oportunidades, pero que la vida era más sencilla y más tranquila. Se queja de la falta de respeto de la juventud actual. Según ella, antes se respetaba más a los padres y a los profesores. "Cuando te regañaban por algo, te regañaban mucho y tenías miedo. Ahora, los chicos ni hacen caso."
>
> Cuando mi abuela era joven, su familia no disponía de teléfono, ni televisor, ni lavadoras. Desde niña, tenía que ayudar con todas las tareas. En el tiempo libre, se escuchaba la radio y se cosía. Después de comer, se echaba la siesta y luego, recuerda mi abuela que solía sentarse con su madre y sus vecinas en el patio a coser, a bordar y a charlar. Cosían y bordaban ropa para los niños, además de cosas para la casa.

Answer the following questions **in English**. You do not need to write in full sentences.

(a) When was the writer's grandmother born?

.... (1)

(b) What was the school leaving age then?

.... (1)

(c) What did Carmen do after she was married?

.... (1)

(d) What is wrong with young people today, according to Carmen?

.... (1)

(e) What did Carmen and her mother use to make while sitting on the patio?

.... (1)

(5 marks)

Do not answer this question yet. You will be asked to come back to it at the end of the unit.

Exam-style question

What worries you most about the future?

Read what these people say about their concerns for the world.

Sofía: Si el ser humano va a sobrevivir, ha de ser optimista y actuar para resolver los problemas más serios. En cuanto al medio ambiente, creo que lo más preocupante es el cambio climático porque será irreversible. Provocará sequías e inundaciones y convertirá muchas regiones del mundo en lugares inhabitables.

Diego: La escasez de agua, en un futuro bastante cercano, presentará un problema enorme para el mundo. Algunos expertos dicen que será el recurso más valioso a finales de este siglo.

Lucía: Debemos buscar soluciones para los millones de personas desplazadas por conflictos como guerras civiles y por desastres naturales. Es uno de los problemas más graves que tendrá que enfrentar nuestra generación y es imprescindible solucionarlo.

Mateo: Acabo de leer que la cantidad de basura en las grandes ciudades del mundo está aumentando y que se duplicará dentro de diez años.

Who says what about global problems? Enter **Sofía**, **Diego**, **Lucía** o **Mateo** in the gaps below. Some names may be used twice or not at all.

Example: _Sofía_____ says that mankind will have to be positive and proactive to safeguard the future of the planet.

(a) .... says that there will not be enough water for the world's population in the near future. (1)

(b) .... fears that climate change will cause extreme and devastating weather. (1)

(c) .... has just found out about an alarming prediction which will affect urban populations. (1)

(d) .... thinks it's essential to find a way of dealing with mass migrations of people. (1)

Answer the following questions **in English**. You do not need to write in full sentences.

(e) According to one of the posts, what will climate change do to many parts of the world?

.... (1)

(f) What, in addition to civil wars, has caused so many refugees to leave their home countries?

.... (1)

(6 marks)

The three key questions in the **skills boosts** will help you improve how you answer these types of questions.

1 How do I use clues from the rubrics, headings and text?

2 How do I use clues from the text surrounding unfamiliar words?

3 How do I recognise parts of unfamiliar words?

① How do I use clues from the rubrics, headings and text?

The heading above a reading task tells you what the text is about. The rubric (instruction line) underneath the heading gives you more information. Read these carefully to establish what the context of the text is before you start to read it. Knowing the context makes it easier to work out the meaning of unfamiliar words and phrases.

① Read the headings and the rubrics from exam texts. Highlight ✎ the words that are the key to the context of each text, as in the example.

Example: Work experience

Read the advertisements on a website for jobs in Spain.

a Protege tu planeta

Lee los consejos para cuidar el medio ambiente.

b Un año académico en Canadá

Lee sobre la experiencia de un estudiante español en el extranjero.

c *Manolito Gafotas* by Elvira Lindo

Read the text about Manolito's day out in Madrid with his grandfather.

d ¿Se puede vivir sin el móvil?

Lee este artículo sobre cómo la tecnología móvil nos cambia la vida.

② **a** Read the extracts and circle Ⓐ the most likely meaning of the highlighted words.

b On paper, explain ✎ how you worked out the answers. Look at the example to help you.

> **20 practical tips for protecting the environment**
>
> Las bombillas LED son de bajo consumo de energía y duran mucho más que las bombillas tradicionales.

Example: batteries   (light bulbs)   fridges

The heading mentions protecting the environment and the text in Spanish says that 'bombillas' LED use less energy, so 'light bulbs' is the most likely meaning.

> **Evento deportivo solidario**
>
> Participa en una caminata nocturna de 5K a la luz de la luna para recaudar fondos para el Hospital de niños.

i   *concert*   *night shift*   *night walk*

> **A school year in Canada**
>
> Mejoré mi nivel de inglés porque estudié en un colegio público y conviví con una familia canadiense.

ii   *got to know*   *lived with*   *studied with*

> **La tecnología móvil es imprescindible**
>
> Si nos encontramos en un sitio muy apartado donde no hay cobertura y no funciona el móvil, sufrimos un ataque de nervios.

iii   *there's no shelter*   *there's no electricity*   *there's no signal*

How do I use clues from the text surrounding unfamiliar words?

When you find a word in a sentence that you don't know, look at the words around it for clues. This will give you an idea of the meaning. Use the tips in the post-it note to help you make sense of the context.

> **A** Look for words you know already in Spanish.
>
> **B** Look at the verbs and the tenses used.
>
> **C** Look for words that are the same or similar in English (cognates and near-cognates).
>
> **D** Look at the words that surround the cognates to see what they connect with.
>
> **E** Look for words that are based on words you might already know in Spanish – e.g. *entretener* (to entertain), *olvidar* (to forget).
>
> **F** Remember that book, film and song titles are shown in italics.

(1) Read the sentences and circle Ⓐ the words that give you clues to the meaning of the highlighted words. Write 🖉 the letter of the tip from the hint box above that helped you.

a La (canción) *Despacito* ha sido el (número uno) en las listas de éxito en más de ochenta países del mundo. _A_

b El guión de la película estaba mal escrito, pero por lo menos los actores eran buenos. ....

c Fuimos a un partido en el Camp Nou y el ambiente en el estadio era fantástico. ....

d Para ir a la boda de mi prima, tuve que llevar traje y corbata. ....

e No ha sido una serie de televisión de alta calidad, pero ha sido muy entretenida. ....

f La música de las bandas sonoras de *Gladiador* y *El Señor de los Anillos* ha llegado a ser música clásica de cine. ....

g Según una encuesta reciente, 60% de los españoles no han leído *El Quijote*. ....

(2) Using the clues you have circled in **(1)**, read the sentences above again and underline Ⓐ the correct meaning of the highlighted words.

a sales lists	record charts	discotheques
b script	casting	special effects
c atmosphere	noise	exciting
d birthday party	house	wedding
e entertaining	boring	disappointing
f bands	sound effects	soundtracks
g despite	although	according to

To make sure your answer is correct, check that the meaning you choose makes sense in the sentence.

3 How do I recognise parts of unfamiliar words?

Looking very carefully at individual words can help you understand their meaning by:
- learning the meaning of common beginnings and endings (prefixes and suffixes)
- spotting the main word within a word (root).

1 Look at the words in bold in these sentences about learning a language abroad. Use the table to help you work out the meaning of the prefixes and write down ✏, on paper, the meaning of the words in English.

Example: *inter/actuar = interact, operate together*

a Sobre todo debes **interactuar** y **convivir** con los demás estudiantes. De esta manera no **malgastarás** el tiempo. No es **imposible** hacer nuevos amigos en el extranjero.

b A veces hay problemas: **anteayer** era **incapaz** de **interrumpir** a un amigo que hablaba muy rápido. Y no me gusta **contradecir** a una persona cuando tengo **insuficiente** vocabulario para explicarme bien.

Prefixes	Meaning
ante-	before
con-/com-/co-	with, together
contra-	against
des-	un-
dis-	not
im-/in-	opposite
inter-	inside, among, between

2 Look at the words in bold in these sentences. Look at the table to help you work out the meaning of the suffix and, on paper, write down ✏ the meaning of the words in English.

Example: *panadero = baker (occupation)*

a El **panadero** era muy **hablador** un **simpaticón**. Su **panadería** estaba en una **callecita encantadora**.

b La **lavadora** no funciona, no encuentro el **secador** y tengo que pasar la **aspiradora** por el **comedor**.

Suffixes	Meaning, use
diminutives	
-ito/-ita, -illo/-illa	little, dear
augmentatives	
-ote /-ota, -ón/ona	big (negative)
-dor/-dora, -tor/-tora, -sor/-sora	verb → noun, occupation, place, adjective
-ario/-aria, ería, -ero/-era, -ista	profession, shop, place, -ary occupation, related to

3 Look at these words and highlight ✏ the root as in the example and try and work out the meaning of each word. Write ✏ the Spanish word it resembles in column A and the English translation of the whole word in the column B.

	A	B
Example: irrepetible	repetir	unrepeatable
a desordenadamente		
b agrandamiento		
c entremetido		
d desilusionante		

Many words are made up of a root plus a suffix and even a prefix: *desproporcionado =* 'disproportionate'. Note that the root word may be slightly modified, but it will still be recognisable.

Your turn!

Here is an exam-style question which requires you to put into practice the skills you have worked on, especially how to make use of the general context and that of the words around the difficult words.

Exam-style question

Volunteering abroad

Read what Nuria has written about her volunteering experiences with a humanitarian charity.

> — □ ×
>
> He estado en Cuba haciendo trabajo voluntario para una ONG que se ocupa del bienestar de la gente más necesitada en los suburbios de La Habana. Llevé donaciones, por ejemplo, pasta de dientes, jabón, maquinillas de afeitar – productos de primera necesidad a los que nosotros estamos muy acostumbrados, pero que en Cuba no son tan fáciles de conseguir. A través de los artículos donados y la ayuda práctica de algunos voluntarios cubanos, la ONG consigue apoyar a personas como Enrique, de 92 años, que no puede salir de su casa por no tener una silla de ruedas. Aunque la pobreza es patente, sorprende la generosidad de los cubanos, que ponen su granito de arena para hacer más tolerable la vida de los desdichados.

Answer the questions **in English.** You do not need to write in full sentences.

(a) What is the work of the charity Nuria volunteered with?

.... (1)

(b) Why did the charity need the items Nuria took with her?

.... (1)

(c) How does the charity help people?

.... (1)

(d) Why couldn't Enrique leave his house?

.... (1)

(e) What did Nuria find surprising?

.... (1)

(5 marks)

- Use the context: look for clues in the heading or in the instructions. The heading and instruction for this question indicate that you can expect to read a person's description of working in a team engaged in some sort of community action in another country.
- Look for clues to understand difficult words in the sentence, for example, an **explanation**. Look for commas, brackets or dashes to indicate an explanation. In the second sentence, the dash after the examples of the donations Nuria took with her will provide you with the answer to question (b).
- Look for phrases such as *por ejemplo* or *como* that provide **examples** that illustrate the word you don't know. Look at the sentence that starts with *A través de los artículos donados...* This sentence provides the answer to question (c) and in the phrase *La ONG consigue apoyar a personas **como** Enrique*, Enrique is the example of the type of person the charity helps. This information will help you work out words like *a través* and *apoyar* which you may not know.
- Look out for words and phrases that introduce contrasting information such as *aunque* and *al contrario*, as they can help you work out the meaning.

Your turn!

Here is another exam-style question which requires you to put into practice the skills you have worked on, specifically how to look carefully at the beginning, middle and end of difficult words to find clues to their meaning. ✏

Exam-style question

Gap year experiences

Read what these students say about their year abroad.

> **Daniel:** Pasé unos meses en Colombia que es el país de mi familia materna. Durante ese tiempo, pude preguntarme si Colombia podría ser un lugar donde instalarme de forma semipermanente. La respuesta fue un rotundo SÍ, pues vi potencial para desarrollar muchos proyectos de futuro.
>
> **Carmen:** Viajar sola es una de las mejores experiencias que he tenido, pues se vive todo mucho más intensamente. Estando lejos valoras todo mucho más, especialmente a los seres queridos que están lejos. Te das cuenta que la distancia no puede separarte de ellos.
>
> **Adrián:** Viajando te das cuenta de la cruda realidad de cómo está el mundo. He visto mucha pobreza, familias que viven con escasos recursos, personas desgastadas trabajando más de 14 horas diarias, niños que en vez de ir al cole mendigan por las calles... Son cosas que no ves en los medios de comunicación.
>
> **Josefa:** Mi nivel de inglés ha sido siempre bastante bueno, pero, aun así, me queda muchísimo por aprender y esto de viajar me ha acelerado el proceso de aprendizaje. Es el idioma por el cual los mochileros se comunican y, sobretodo, hablándolo te echas muchos amigos de todo el mundo.

(a) Who says what about their year abroad? Enter either **Daniel**, **Carmen**, **Adrián** or **Josefa** in the gaps below. Some names may be used twice or not at all.

Example: _Daniel_ says that the visit abroad was a chance to see if there might be work opportunities there.

(i) .... tells us travelling encourages you to appreciate things and people. **(1)**

(ii) .... mentions that travelling teaches you about real life in other countries. **(1)**

(iii) .... mentions that missing friends and family makes you realise how close you are to them. **(1)**

(iv) .... says that you come across things you don't see on TV. **(1)**

(b) Answer the following questions **in English**. You do not need to write in full sentences.

(i) According to one of the posts, why is being able to speak a common language so important when meeting other travellers? **(1)**

....

(ii) According to another post, what is the benefit of not travelling with other friends? **(1)**

....

(6 marks)

Review your skills

Check up

Check your responses to the exam-style questions on pages 71 and 72. Tick ✓ the column that shows how well you think you have done each of the following.

	Not quite ✓	Nearly there ✓	Got it! ✓
used clues from the rubrics, headings and text	☐	☐	☐
used clues from the text surrounding unfamiliar words	☐	☐	☐
recognised parts of unfamiliar words	☐	☐	☐

Need more practice?

Go back to pages 66 and 67 and complete ✐ the two exam-style questions there. Use the checklist to help you.

Checklist In my answers, do I...	✓
read the rubrics and the headings to find information that will help me understand the text?	
notice the titles of books or films in italics?	
look for words I already know in Spanish surrounding the words I don't know?	
look for cognates and near-cognates?	
work out the meaning of unfamiliar words because they're based on words I already know?	
look at the roots, prefixes and suffixes of unfamiliar words to work out their meaning?	

How confident do you feel about each of these **skills**? Colour in ✐ the bars.

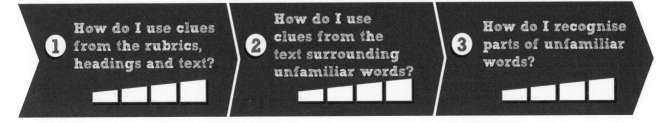

1 How do I use clues from the rubrics, headings and text?

2 How do I use clues from the text surrounding unfamiliar words?

3 How do I recognise parts of unfamiliar words?

Answers

Unit 1

Page 2

① Prefiero

me encanta

Me gustan

Prefiero

Me encanta

Me lo paso (bomba)

Para mí es (importante)

es (divertido)

Page 3

② Places: castillo, estadio, playa, albergue

Activities: comprar la entrada ver el partido, comprar comida tomar un refresco, tomar el sol, ducharme, comprar recuerdos

Page 4

① a I, b D, c J, d A, e L, f F, g H, h B, i E, j G, k C, l K

② **a** viajar   **d** coche

b castillo   **e** perder

c comprar

③ **a** Lucia: tengo miedo de volar

Julio: media pensión

Beatriz: más barato

Marcos: frío, nieve, esquiar

b i Beatriz

ii Lucía

iii Marcos

iv Julio

Page 5

① **a** ii <u>partido</u> – sports match, <u>comprar</u> – buy, <u>entradas</u> – tickets

iii <u>comprar</u> – buy, <u>crema solar</u> – sun protection, <u>playa</u> – beach, <u>quemarse</u> – burn

iv <u>perder</u> – lose, <u>pasaporte & cartera</u> – passport and wallet (valuables), <u>desastre</u> – disaster (negative reaction)

iv <u>alojamiento</u> – lodging, <u>piscina & restaurantes</u> – swimming pool and restaurants (amenities)

vi <u>plano & folleto</u> – map and brochure (tourist information), <u>lugares de interés</u> – touristy places

b A ii, B i, C vi, D iv, E v

Page 6

① **a** about

b for

c for

d from

e in

② **a** ii

b i

c ii

Page 7

Exam-style question

(a) Carlota, (b) Daniel, (c) Gabriela, (d) Daniel, (e) Alejandro, (f) Carlota

Page 8

Exam-style question

(a) clothes shop, (b) supermarket, (c) bike hire, (d) museum, (e) garage

Page 9

Page 2 exam-style question

(a) Juan

(b) Miguel

(c) Juan

(d) Susana

(e) Amelia

(f) Susana

Page 3 exam-style question

(a) stadium

(b) supermarket

(c) bar

(d) hostel

(e) souvenir shop

Unit 2

Page 10

① Cognates: intimidación, sociales, representa, conclusión, víctimas, constante, parte

Near-cognates: silencio, casos, compañeros, estudiantes, intimidados, acusan, agresores, conscientes, ocurre

False friends: profesores, patio

Page 12

② A club, judo, opinión, participar, competiciones, nacionales, parte, importante, actividad, noviembre, trofeo

B uniforme, instituto, formal, limita, individualidad, práctico, diferencias, económicas, estudiantes, obvias

C necesarias, ejemplo, permite, usar, móvil, clase, prohibido, agresivo, puntual

3 a i foto, gimnasia

ii geografía, estudiamos, contaminación

iii excursión, estadio, Olímpicos

iv trofeo, esquí, España

v estrés, fenomenal

b i foto = photo, gimnasia = gymnasium

ii geografía = geography, estudiamos = we study, contaminación = contamination/pollution

iii excursión = excursion, estadio = stadium, Olímpicos = Olympics

iv trofeo = trophy, esquí = ski, España = Spain

v estrés = stress, fenomenal = phenomenal/great

Page 13

1 a [6] El profesor de educación de física es estricto y no tiene paciencia, pero controla bien la clase.

The PE (physical education) teacher is strict and he has no patience, but he controls the class well.

b [4] Tengo que admitir que me gusta estudiar historia y geografía.

I have to admit that I like studying history and geography.

c [4] La nota es para informar a mis padres que iré al club de fotografía mañana.

The note is to inform my parents that I'm going to the photography club tomorrow.

d [4] Voy a decidir si participar en el concurso de teatro es buena idea o no.

I'm going to decide if participating in the theatre/drama competition is a good idea or not.

e [3] Desafortunadamente el uniforme de mi colegio en primaria era feo.

Unfortunately, the uniform in my primary school was ugly.

f [4] Para hacer esta actividad es necesario poner atención y aprender el vocabulario.

In order to do this activity it's necessary to pay attention and learn the vocabulary.

g [3] En mi insti no hay mucha intimidación ni violencia entre los estudiantes.

In my school there isn't much intimidation/ bullying or violence among the students.

h [3] Tengo la oportunidad de participar en un intercambio y visitar a mi amigo español.

I have the opportunity to participate in an exchange and visit my Spanish friend.

i [4] Estoy estudiando para el examen de biología. Tengo que escribir sobre un experimento.

I am studying for the biology exam. I have to write about an experiment.

j [3] Mi compañero no es estúpido; es muy inteligente, pero es muy tímido.

My classmate isn't stupid; he's very intelligent, but he's timid/shy.

2

Spanish	English	Examples from sentences
English verbs ending in consonant, add –ar or -ir		controlar/control
		admitir/admit
		visitar/visit
-ar or -ir	-e	admirar/admire
		decidir/decide
Nouns or adjectives ending in -encia	-ence	violencia/violence
		paciencia /patience
-ario	-ary	necesario/necessary
		vocabulario/vocabulary
		primario/primary
-ción	-tion	intimidación/intimidation
		atención/attention
		educación/education
		competición/competition
-dad	-ty	posibilidad/possibility
		actividad/activity
-ía/-ia/-ío/-io	-y	historia/history
		geografía/geography
		fotografía/photography
		biología/biology
English nouns nouns and adjectives ending in consonant, add –o/a or -e		inteligente/intelligent
		tímido/timid
		estúpido/stupid
		experimento/experiment
		clase/class
		nota/note
		física/physical
		uniforme/uniform
		estudiante/student
Adverbs ending in -mente	-ly	desafortunadamente/ unfortunately

3 teatro = theatre

estudiante = student

desafortunadamente = unfortunately

examen = exam

inteligente = intelligent

estúpido = stupid

Page 14

1 a Mi amigo es una persona sensible y le disgustan las discusiones en el patio.

My friend is a sensitive person and he is upset by arguments in the playground.

b La comida del insti es bastante sana, pero las sopas son saladas y por lo tanto siempre bebo un vaso de agua.

The food at school is quite healthy but the soups are salty and therefore I always drink a glass of water.

c) Mi profesora <u>envía</u> cartas a casa si no somos <u>educados</u>.

My teacher sends letters home if we are not polite.

d) No <u>recuerdo</u> dónde está la <u>parada</u> de autobús <u>escolar</u>.

I don't remember where the school bus stop is.

e) Voy a <u>realizar</u> una <u>encuesta</u> para ver cuántas personas <u>asisten</u> a los clubs extraescolares.

I'm going to carry out a survey about how many people attend the extracurricular activities.

2) a) actual = at the moment

b) atender = pay attention

c) campo = countryside/field

d) constiparse = to catch a cold

e) chocar = to crash

f) una desgracia = misfortune

g) embarazada = pregnant

h) reunión = meeting

Page 15

Exam-style question

(a) (i) every term

(ii) two years

(iii) playing with other people

(b) (i) in the municipal/town sports centre

(ii) to win a trophy

Page 16

Exam-style question

(a) he started to get used to the differences between the two countries (look for 'acostumbrarme' = to get accustomed/used to, 'diferencias' = differences; don't be led astray by 'al principio' = at the beginning, not in principal or 'disgustaba' = upset, not disgusted)

(b) that British pupils can't wear their own clothes/have to wear a uniform (look for 'curiosa' = curious/strange, 'alumnos' = alumni/pupils, and in the next sentence the mention of 'uniforme' = uniform. Careful with 'ropa' = clothes, not rope)

(c) any summary that conveys the point that on an exchange you learn about life in another country (look for 'recomiendo' = I recommend, 'diaria' = daily, 'costumbres' = customs)

Page 17

Page 10 exam-style question

(a) 1 in 4 cases

(b) girls

(c) any summary that conveys the point that victims of bullying are no longer silent

Page 11 exam-style question

(a) (i) they are not adequate

(ii) sports science

(iii) old labs

(b) (i) maths teacher

(ii) trips/cinema

Unit 3

Page 18

1) A negative view: señores … antipáticos, niños traviesos, un perro muy desobediente

Page 20

1)
a)	tengo que	debo
b)	a menudo	frecuentemente
c)	fiel	leal
d)	desafortunadamente	desgraciadamente
e)	usar	utilizar
f)	dar una vuelta	dar un paseo
g)	un e-mail	un correo electrónico
h)	el ordenador	el portátil
i)	el teléfono	el móvil
j)	lo bueno de	la ventaja de
k)	se puede	es posible

2)
a)	<u>Se utilizan</u>	Se usan
	<u>gratuito</u>	gratis
b)	<u>se puede</u>	es posible
	<u>el teléfono</u>	el móvil
	<u>el portátil</u>	el ordenador
c)	<u>Desgraciadamente</u>	Desafortunadamente
d)	<u>Debes</u>	Tienes que
	<u>un correo electrónico</u>	un e-mail

Page 21

1) A c, B a, C d, D b

2)
	a)	b)
we argue	nos peleamos	nos llevamos bien
optimistic	optimista	pesimista
friendly	simpático	antipático
patient	paciente	impaciente

3) a) F b) J c) L d) F e) J f) M g) L

Page 22

1) a) i leisure activities

ii weather

iii physical description

iv food

b) i biografías, novelas, ciencia ficción, historias de vampiros

ii hace mucho viento, hace sol, va a llover

iii guapa, alta, delgada, pelo moreno, largo y ondulado, ojos marrones

iv de primer plato, ensalada, mariscos, gazpacho, de segundo, pollo, a la brasa, gambas, de postre, flan, helado, fruta

(2) (a) i B

ii A

(b) Este modelo es el más <u>rápido</u> con una velocidad máxima de <u>200 kilómetros por hora</u>. Además, es el más lujoso y más <u>cómodo</u> de la nueva serie. Debajo de los <u>asientos de detrás</u>, hay un cajón especial para poner los portátiles, el monedero, los móviles o las cámaras.

Acabamos de salir del <u>estadio</u>. ¡El <u>partido</u> fue fantástico! Vamos a coger un taxi porque está lloviendo y hay muchísima gente haciendo cola para entrar al metro – incluyendo los hinchas del otro <u>equipo</u>, ¡todos de mal humor por la derrota!

(3) (a) a speed

(b) a box

(c) the supporters

(d) the defeat

Page 23

(1) Sabelotodo – general knowledge

Organízate – personal organisation

Lengua mundo – languages

Exam-style question

(a) Organízate

(b) En forma

(c) Lengua mundo

(d) Sabelotodo

(e) Organízate

(f) En forma

Page 24

Exam-style question

(a) (i) a good friend must be loyal

(ii) because he's funny and he makes her laugh

(b) (i) they are very different

(ii) Daniel

(iii) he likes loud rock music and she doesn't, she likes reading science fiction while Daniel prefers stories about vampires

Page 25

Page 18 exam-style question

(a) unfriendly

(b) badly behaved

(c) fifteen

(d) sporty

(e) reading

Page 19 exam-style question

(i) B

(ii) B

(iii) D

(iv) A

(v) B

Unit 4

Page 26

(1) Quién – who

Qué – what

Cómo – how

Cuáles – which

Dónde – where

Page 27

(2) (d)

Page 28

(1) (a) what

(b) who

(c) when

(d) where

(e) how much

(f) how

(g) which

(h) why

(2) (a) a place

(b) a choice

(c) a person

(d) a reason

(e) a number

(f) a time

(g) an activity

(3) (a) b (b) e c a d f (e) g (f) c (g) d

Page 29

(1)

(a)	What kind of <u>work</u> does Natalia Tena do?	actriz y cantante
(b)	<u>Where</u> is she <u>from</u>?	Londres, nacionalidad británica
(c)	How many <u>languages</u> does she speak?	inglés, español, vasco
(d)	Which part of Spain is her <u>father from</u>?	País Vasco / norte de España
(e)	Which <u>instrument</u> does Natalia play?	el acordeón
(f)	Which <u>TV series</u> has she appeared in?	Juego de tronos

(2) (a) She's an actress and a singer.

(b) She's from London. She's British.

(c) She speaks three languages.

(d) Her father is from the Basque country in the north of Spain.

(e) She plays the acordeon.

(f) She's appeared in *Game of Thrones*.

(3) Lorena: Lo que más me gusta es salir con mis amigos a dar una vuelta, a charlar y pasar el rato.

Carlos: Toco el teclado y me encanta escuchar todo tipo de música, especialmente la electrónica.

Nina: Me gusta el deporte. Juego al fútbol y al voleibol. ¡Me gusta ganar!

Manolo: No soy teleadicto, pero para descansar, me encanta ver comedias y series policíacas.

(a) Nina

(b) Manolo

(c) Lorena

(d) Carlos

(e) Manolo

(f) Nina

Page 30

(1) **(a)** i lista de los grupos, sitios públicos, Internet

ii festival, del 27 al 29 de abril

iii entrada, 65 euros, dormir

iv no quieres llevar, organizaión, alquila, pocos euros

v Los Locos y Kaos Urbano, más de 140 grupos

(b) i posters

ii takes place

iii camping

iv tent

v are headlining

(2) **(a)** emocionantes

(b) decepcionado

(c) escalofriante

(d) impresionante

(3) **(a)** (más, las comedias, las pelis de amor) Action and adventure films are likely to be 'exciting'.

(b) (quedaste, no era tan bueno) The last episode wasn't as good as the previous ones so Juan was 'disappointed'.

(c) (película de terror, miedo) A horror film is likely to be 'frightening / chilling'.

(d) (originales personajes, estilo ágil) The recent novel has good characters and style, so it's 'impressive'.

Page 31

Exam-style question

(a) morning

(b) four

(c) swim

(d) Mondays

(e) free

Page 32

Exam-style question

(a) being healthier in the future

(b) 30 minutes to an hour

(c) avoiding obesity and depression; being disciplined; being able to work as part of a team, respect others and follow rules

Page 33

Page 26 exam-style question

(a) paseo

(b) móvil

(c) chicas

(d) bicicleta

(e) casa

Page 27 exam-style question

(a) Diario deportivo

(b) Gran Hermano

(c) La vida de los animales

(d) Cocineros de primera

(e) Diario deportivo

Unit 5

Page 36

(1) **(a)** Cristina y yo compramos, yo prefiero

(b) estoy yo, Rafa y Tomás quieren

(c) Rafa, Tomás y yo vamos

(d) Rafa, Tomás y yo fuimos

(e) la comida no costaba

(f) Rafa y Tomás probarán

(2) **(a)** C: subject of verb – 'compró un monedero' (she bought a purse), 'compré un vestido' (I bought a dress, ie clothes, the Spanish for which is 'ropa')

(b) A: Preferir & gustar are synonyms, los grandes almacenes = subject of verb preferir

(c) D: Voy = first person therefore refers to Aurora, hace = third person therefore refers to mother, and complement 'en línea' (= por Internet)

Page 37

(1) i (3rd person plural, present) They are so cold.

ii (3rd person plural, present) They are always open.

iii (3rd person plural future) They (the shops) will be shut.

(2) **(a)** i Hacía, hubo, sorprendió ii prefería comimos

(b) i imperfect ii imperfect

(c) i C ii D

Page 38

(1) Quise comprar unas botas nuevas para el invierno. La zapatería estaba en la calle principal pero no la encontraba. Pedí direcciones a un hombre y me contestó: "No la encontrarás abierta, mejor ir a los grandes almacenes." Tomé un autobús que me llevó allí. Una dependienta me preguntó qué quería. Le contesté que quería unas botas. "No las tenemos ahora porque es verano," me contestó. "¿Qué me recomienda?" le pregunté. Al final, me compré unas sandalias.

② **a** Yo le doy la entrada y él la da el dinero.

b Ellas los buscan y él lo compra.

c Nosotras lo apreciamos, pero a ellas les gusta más.

d Él se lo dio, pero ellos no lo miraron.

Page 39

Exam-style question

(a) some documents

(b) by bus

(c) any of the following: listening to music, reading, studying, talking to his friends

(d) he walked

Page 40

Exam-style question

(i) D, (ii) C, (iii) B, (iv) B, (v) A

Page 41

Page 34 exam-style question

(a) Sunday

(b) Alejandro

(c) in the middle of the street

(d) The boots were still OK (useful). / He didn't like to throw anything away.

Page 35 exam-style question

(i) D, (ii) B, (iii) B, (iv) A, (v) C

Unit 6

Page 43

① Questions 1 and 2 require the exact information; question 3 requires some deduction.

Page 44

① **a** i She normally stays at home, but not always and not this coming New Year.

ii Wrong, the question asks 'how' she is spending New Year, not 'what' she does at New Year.

iii Could work but ambiguous, she will be there at the time.

iv Correct answer

b i Wrong, question is asking what food he likes to cook the most, not which meal of the day.

ii Wrong, he cooks these among other things, but not the most.

iii Correct answer

iv Contradicts the text, he says he doesn't like eggs.

Page 45

① **a** Difficult to make a paella in the street for so many people.

b Because they were more spectacular.

c The last/final night.

Page 46

① **a** en salas de toda España

b Para conseguir precios reducidos se debe registrar en la página web www.fiestadelcine.com

c en las taquillas de los cines participantes y por Internet

d medio millón más que el año pasado

e a pesar de que competirá con la celebración de los partidos de semifinales de la Liga de Campeones de fútbol los últimos dos días

② **a** It's the biggest in Spain ~~and lasts 3 days~~.
The question is not about how long the festival lasts.

b They come from all over the world ~~to demonstrate their skills~~.
The question is not about what they have come to do.

c sports skills ~~at the hands of the experts~~
The question doesn't ask about who teaches in the workshops.

③ **a** all over Spain

b reduced ticket price

c cinema box offices and online

d half a million

e (Champions League semi-finals) football matches

Page 47

Exam-style question

(a) (i) the whole family

(ii) the first star

(iii) talk in human language

(b) (i) go to church

(ii) sweets or money

Page 48

Exam-style question

(a) in his town ('en mi pueblo')

(b) eating (so much) meat ('comer tanta carne')

(c) Any summary that conveys the point that we can buy cheaper unbranded, local products and replace some of our meat consumption with vegetarian meals.

Page 49

Page 42 exam-style question

(a) (i) train station

(ii) friendly

(iii) French

(b) (i) two

(ii) lunch

Page 43 exam-style question

(a) He made her a card.

(b) She loved it (more than all the other presents).

(c) Any summary that conveys the point that you don't need to spend a lot of money on a present to give pleasure.

Unit 7

Page 52

① **a** P   **b** N   **c** P   **d** P
e N   **f** P   **g** N   **h** P
i N   **j** P   **k** P   **l** N

② A   aprender – **e** to learn ✓
B   aburrirse – **a** to be bored ✗
C   ayudar – **c** to help ✓
D   ganar (dinero) – **b** to earn (money) ✓
E   mejorar – **d** to improve ✓
F   viajar – **f** to travel ✓

③ **a** El sueldo es muy alto pero tienes que trabajar muchas horas.
b El horario es flexible y lo bueno es que tienes los fines de semana libres.
c El jefe es bastante severo pero nos explica bien las tareas.
d El trabajo no era difícil pero llegó a ser monótono.
e Lo mejor de las prácticas fue que aprendí mucho. Fue una experiencia útil.
f Gané muy poco dinero pero mejoré mi nivel de español.
g El trabajo no era interesante. Fue una pérdida de tiempo.

Page 53

① **a** Creo que es importante aprender idiomas.
b Nuestros profesores piensan que vale la pena hacer prácticas laborales.
c En mi opinión, no es necesario pasar la aspiradora todos los días.
d Mi abuelo dice que no importa qué haces, sino cómo lo haces.
e Para mí, lo más importante es hacer un trabajo útil.

② **a** una desventaja
b vale la pena
c desafortunadamente
d una buena idea
e Admiro

③ **a** He loves his work. ✓
b He thinks playing sport helps students to learn how to follow rules. ✗
c He gets job satisfaction from seeing positive results. ✓
d He thinks that sport is beneficial for young people. ✓
e He doesn't like teaching students who don't like sport. ✗
f He finds that only a small number of students have a negative attitude. ✓

Page 54

① **a** ii   (trabajar de dependienta) work as a saleswoman
iii   (activa) active (desportista) sporty (voy a ser o profesora o maestra) I'm going to be a teacher
iv   (quiero trabajar en turismo) I want to work in tourism (Domino el inglés y el francés) I'm fluent in English and French
v   (me encanta cocinar) I love cooking
vi   (Prefiero el campo a la ciudad) I prefer the countryside to the city (Quiero trabajar al aire libre) I want to work outside

b A Un hotel en Ibiza
Buscamos personal de cocina (v) para trabajar en el restaurante. Debes tener buen nivel de dos o más idiomas (iv). Experiencia en el mundo de la restauración será una ventaja.

B Grandes almacenes deportivos
Tienda (ii) de ropa y equipo deportivo busca jóvenes para trabajar de mediados de julio a finales de agosto. Necesitas buena presencia y aptitudes de comunicación con los clientes.

C Campamento de verano
Se buscan monitores para trabajar en un entorno natural (vi) para este verano. No necesitas experiencia, pero debes tener una personalidad abierta y positiva. Vivirás en el campamento y animarás a los niños a participar en actividades deportivas (iii) y creativas.

D Empresa de marketing
Buscamos a dos jóvenes para realizar tareas administrativas durante el verano. No hace falta tener experiencia de trabajar en una oficina, pero se requieren conocimientos de Word, Photoshop y Excel (i).

c i D   ii B   iii C   iv A   v A   vi C

Page 55

Exam-style question

(a) Taking a gap year is relatively new in Spain.
(b) She improved her English. / She became more independent and responsible.
(c) Taking a gap year enables students to find out about other cultures and to learn languages. It also helps them to improve their communication skills, to be more adaptable, to work as part of a team and to be more open-minded.

Page 56

Exam-style question

(a) (i)   working as a shop assistant and selling clothes
(ii)   to fill in for permanent staff who are away on holiday
(iii)   you get discounts on clothes / you will have to work at weekends
(b) (i)   teenagers who are at least 16
(ii)   the work is varied / you can see films for free / you don't get paid much

Page 57

Page 50 exam-style question

(a) Empresa de marketing

(b) Campamento de verano

(c) Un hotel en Ibiza

(d) Campamento de verano

(e) Un hotel en Ibiza

Page 51 exam-style question

(i) B

(ii) D

(iii) C

(iv) A

(v) D

Unit 8

Page 59

① (a) <u>They</u> took part <u>more of</u> 50 people.

(b) It was quite cold and it was <u>windy, but</u> we had a good time.

(c) Af<u>t</u>erwards, we all had breakfast in the <u>bar of the village</u>.

(d) We're going to do the race again <u>the year coming</u>.

Page 60

① (a) (hace dos semanas) We went on a trip to the mountains two weeks ago.

(b) (demasiada) In the big cities, there are too many homeless people.

(c) (demasiado) Drinking too much alcohol is quite a serious problem.

(d) (mucho) Taking drugs is much more dangerous.

② (a) Me encanta el deporte y normalmente practico algún deporte todos los días. Casi nunca veo la tele porque es aburrido, pero hace poco vi un campeonato de atletismo en que una atleta de mi región ganó una medalla. Fue muy emocionante. El año que viene me gustaría participar en un triatlón.

(b) I love sport and I usually do some kind of sport nearly every day. I hardly ever watch TV because it's boring, but a little while ago, I watched an athletics championship in which an athlete from my area won a medal. It was very exciting. I would like to take part in a triathlon next year.

Page 61

① (a) I think the most worrying problem is the climate change.

(b) We should encourage to everyone to recycle more.

(c) I go to the school by bike or on foot every day.

(d) We have just of read an interesting report about renewable energy.

(e) You shouldn't throw litter onto the ground.

(f) The pollution of the air in big cities is a serious problem.

(g) You should protect animals in danger of extinction.

② (a) I live in an industrial city to the north of Barcelona.

(b) The environmental problem that worries me most is air pollution.

(c) There are too many cars in the city centre.

(d) We should use public transport or go on foot.

(e) We must inform the public about the importance of looking after the environment.

Page 62

① (a) En casa hacemos todo lo posible para ahorrar energía. En invierno, sólo usamos la calefacción cuando hace mucho frío. En verano, cerramos las cortinas y las persianas durante el día y la casa se queda fresca por dentro. De esta manera, sólo usamos los ventiladores únicamente cuando hace mucho calor. Además, tenemos placas solares en el tejado para calentar el agua.

(b) i heating   We use it only when it's cold.

ii blinds   We keep them closed to keep the house cool.

iii fans   We use them only when it's very hot.

iv solar panels   They heat the water.

v roof   Solar panels are usually on the roof.

② (a) Voy a comer más ensalada, verduras y fruta.

I'm going to eat more salad, ~~leaves~~ and fruit. (green vegetables)

(b) Me gustan las manzanas, pero no me gustan las peras.

I like apples, but I don't like ~~hot dogs~~. (pears)

(c) Vivimos en un barrio en las afueras de la ciudad y hay mucho tráfico.

We live in a ~~bar~~ in the outskirts of the city and there is a lot of traffic. (neighbourhood)

(d) Hay que apagar las luces para ahorrar energía.

We must ~~switch on~~ the lights to save energy. (switch off)

Page 63

Exam-style question

I think paralympic athletes are good role models for children and young people because they have to fight to overcome many difficulties. Also, I think it's worthwhile taking part in charity events. Recently, I volunteered at a cycle race in my area that raised money for homeless people. It was a very positive experience.

Page 64

Exam-style question

Two months ago, I changed my job and now I haven't got time to go to the gym or the swimming pool. To relax, I started smoking but now I need to change my routine to have a healthier lifestyle. I think that, from Monday to Friday, I'm going to get up earlier to go running before going to the office. I'm going to change my diet and eat more salad, green vegetables and fruit. In addition, I'm going to stop smoking.

Page 65

Page 58 exam-style question

I live in a small town in the north of Spain. I like swimming and I like gymastics. Last year, I went on holiday to France with my parents, my sister, my uncle and aunt and my cousins. We went by car and it was quite a long journey but we had a great time. This year, I'm going (/ I will go) to a summer camp in the mountains with my sister.

Page 59 exam-style question

In February, we organised a charity bicycle race in my village. More than 50 people took part. It was quite cold and it was windy but, despite the bad weather, we had a good time. Afterwards we all ate breakfast in the village bar. We're going to do the race again next year.

Unit 9

Page 68

1
a Protege tu planeta

Lee los consejos para cuidar el medio ambiente.

b Un año académico en Canadá

Lee sobre la experiencia de un estudiante español en el extranjero.

c Manolito Gafotas by Elvira Lindo

Read the text about Manolito's day out in Madrid with his grandfather.

d ¿Se puede vivir sin el móvil?

Lee este artículo sobre cómo la tecnología móvil nos cambia la vida.

2
a i night walk
ii lived with
iii there's no signal

b Students' own answers.

Page 69

1
a El guión de la película estaba mal escrito, pero por lo menos los actores eran buenos. A

b Fuimos a un partido en el Camp Nou y el ambiente en el estadio era fantástico. A

c Para ir a la boda de mi prima, tuve que llevar traje y corbata. A

d No ha sido una serie de televisión de alta calidad, pero ha sido muy entretenida. E

e La música de las bandas sonoras de Gladiador y El Señor de los Anillos ha llegado a ser música clásica de cine. F

f Según una encuesta reciente, 60% de los españoles no han leído El Quijote. C

2
a record charts
b script
c atmosphere
d wedding
e entertaining
f soundtracks
g according to

Page 70

1
a inter/actuar = interact, con/vivir = live with, mal/gastarás = you will waste, im/posible = impossible

b ante/ayer = the day before yesterday, in/capaz = incapable, inter/rumpir = interrupt, contra/decir = contradict, in/suficiente = insufficient

2
a panadero = baker (occupation), hablador = talkative (verb → adjective) simpaticón = very friendly (augmentative), panadería = bakery (shop), callecita = little street (diminutive), encantadora = charming (verb → adjective),

b lavadora = washing machine (verb → noun), secador = (hair) dryer (verb → noun) aspiradora = vacuum cleaner (verb → noun) comedor = dining room (verb → place)

3
a desordenadamente = orden = disorderly
b agrandamiento = grande = enlargement
c entremetido = meter = meddling, intruding
d desilusionante = ilusión = disillusioning, disappointing

Page 71

Exam-style question

(a) helping the most needy (in Havana)

(b) They aren't easy to get in Cuba.

(c) It supports people with donated items and practical help.

(d) because he didn't have a wheelchair

(e) the generosity of the Cuban people

Page 72

Exam-style question

(a) Carmen

(b) Adrián

(c) Carmen

(d) Adrián

(e) because it's a way of making friends

(f) every experience is more intense

Page 73

Page 66 exam-style question

(a) in the 1940s

(b) 14

(c) looked after her house and her children

(d) they don't show respect

(e) clothes for the children / things for the house

Page 67 exam-style question

(a) Diego

(b) Sofía

(c) Mateo

(d) Lucía

(e) make them uninhabitable

(f) natural disasters

Notes